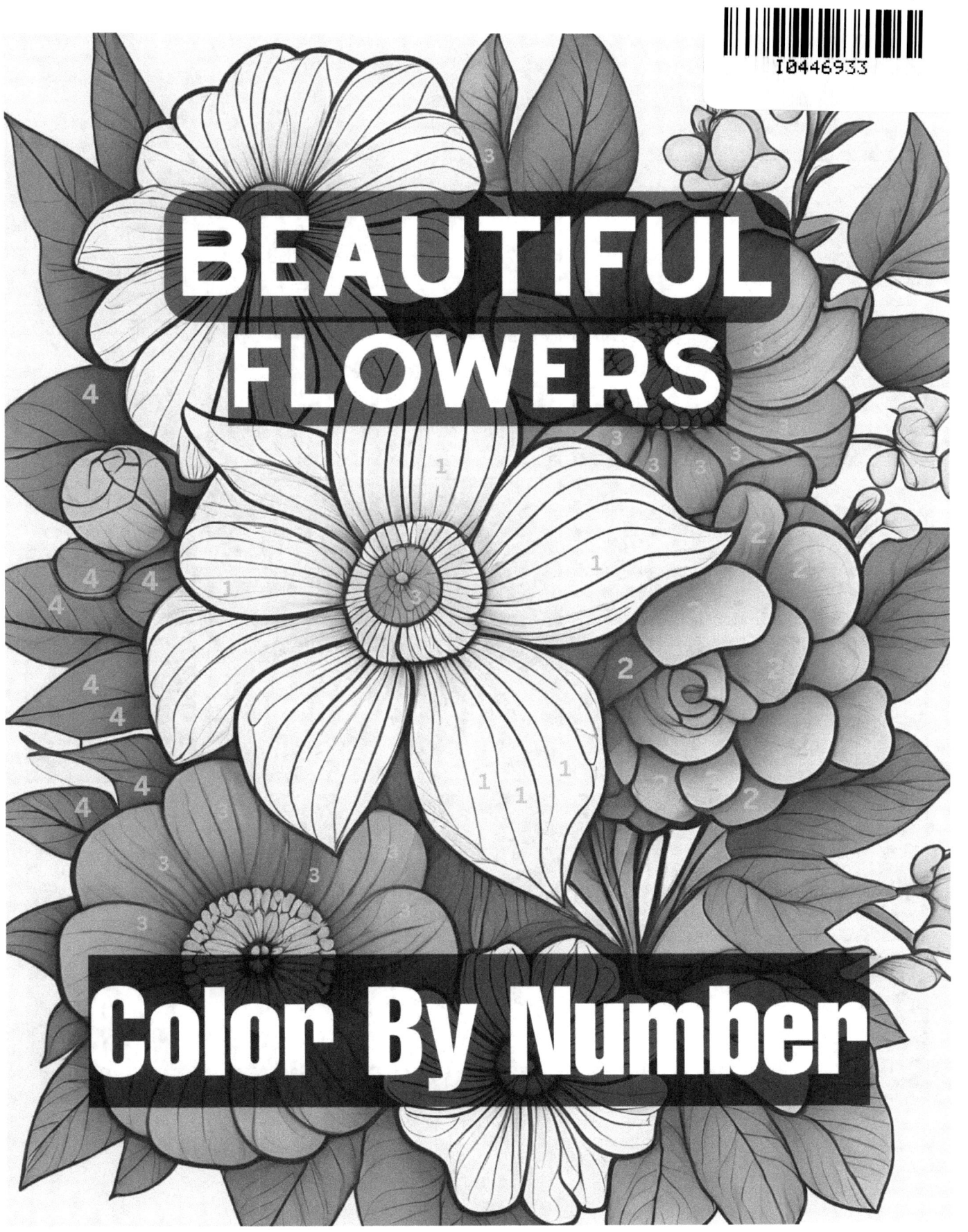

BEAUTIFUL FLOWERS

Color By Number

I0446933

1 WHITE	2 LIGHT YELLOW	3 MEDIUM YELLOW	4 DARK YELLOW	5 YELLOW ORANGE
6 LIGHT ORANGE	7 MEDIUM ORANGE	8 DARK ORANGE	9 ORANGE RED	10 PINK
11 MEDIUM RED	12 DARK RED	13 LIGHT GREEN	14 MEDIUM GREEN	15 DARK GREEN
16 GREEN BLUE	17 LIGHT BLUE	18 MEDIUM BLUE	19 DARK BLUE	20 BLUE PURPLE
21 LIGHT PURPLE	22 MEDIUM PURPLE	23 DARK PURPLE	24 LIGHT BROWN	25 MEDIUM BROWN
26 DARK BROWN	27 LIGHT GRAY	28 MEDIUM GRAY	29 DARK GRAY	30 BLACK

CUSTOM COLOR CHART

1. _____

2. _____

3. _____

4. _____

5. _____

6. _____

7. _____

8. _____

9. _____

10. _____

11. _____

12. _____

13. _____

14. _____

15. _____

16. _____

17. _____

18. _____

19. _____

20. _____

21. _____

22. _____

23. _____

24. _____

25. _____

26. _____

27. _____

28. _____

29. _____

30. _____

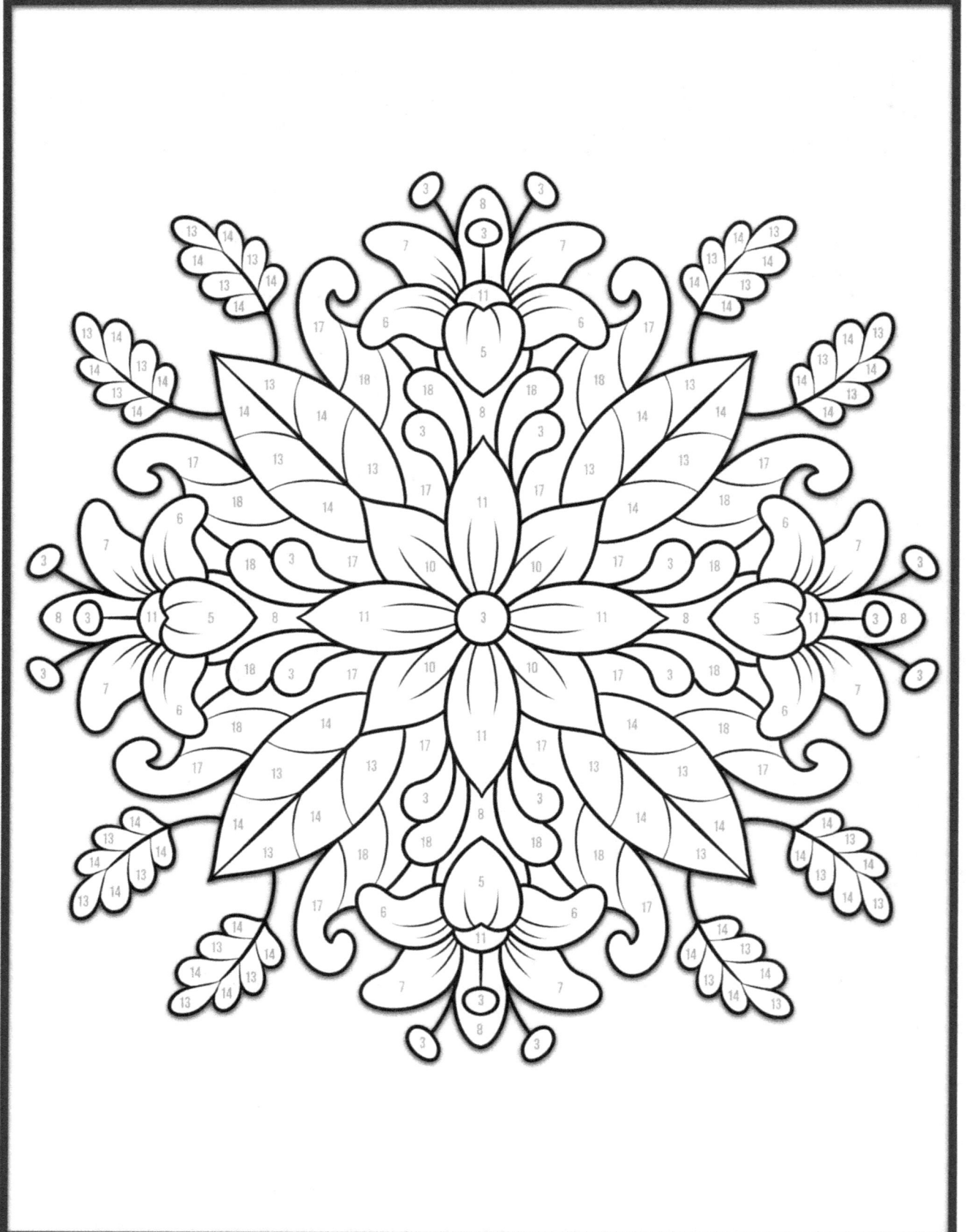

CUSTOM COLOR CHART

1. WHITE

2. LIGHT YELLOW

3. MEDIUM YELLOW

4. DARK YELLOW

5. YELLOW ORANGE

6. LIGHT ORANGE

7. MEDIUM ORANGE

8. DARK ORANGE

9. ORANGE RED

10. PINK

11. MEDIUM RED

12. DARK RED

13. LIGHT GREEN

14. MEDIUM GREEN

15. DARK GREEN

16. GREEN BLUE

17. LIGHT BLUE

18. MEDIUM BLUE

19. DARK BLUE

20. BLUE PURPLE

21. LIGHT PURPLE

22. MEDIUM PURPLE

23. DARK PURPLE

24. LIGHT BROWN

25. MEDIUM BROWN

26. DARK BROWN

27. LIGHT GRAY

28. MEDIUM GRAY

29. DARK GRAY

30. BLACK

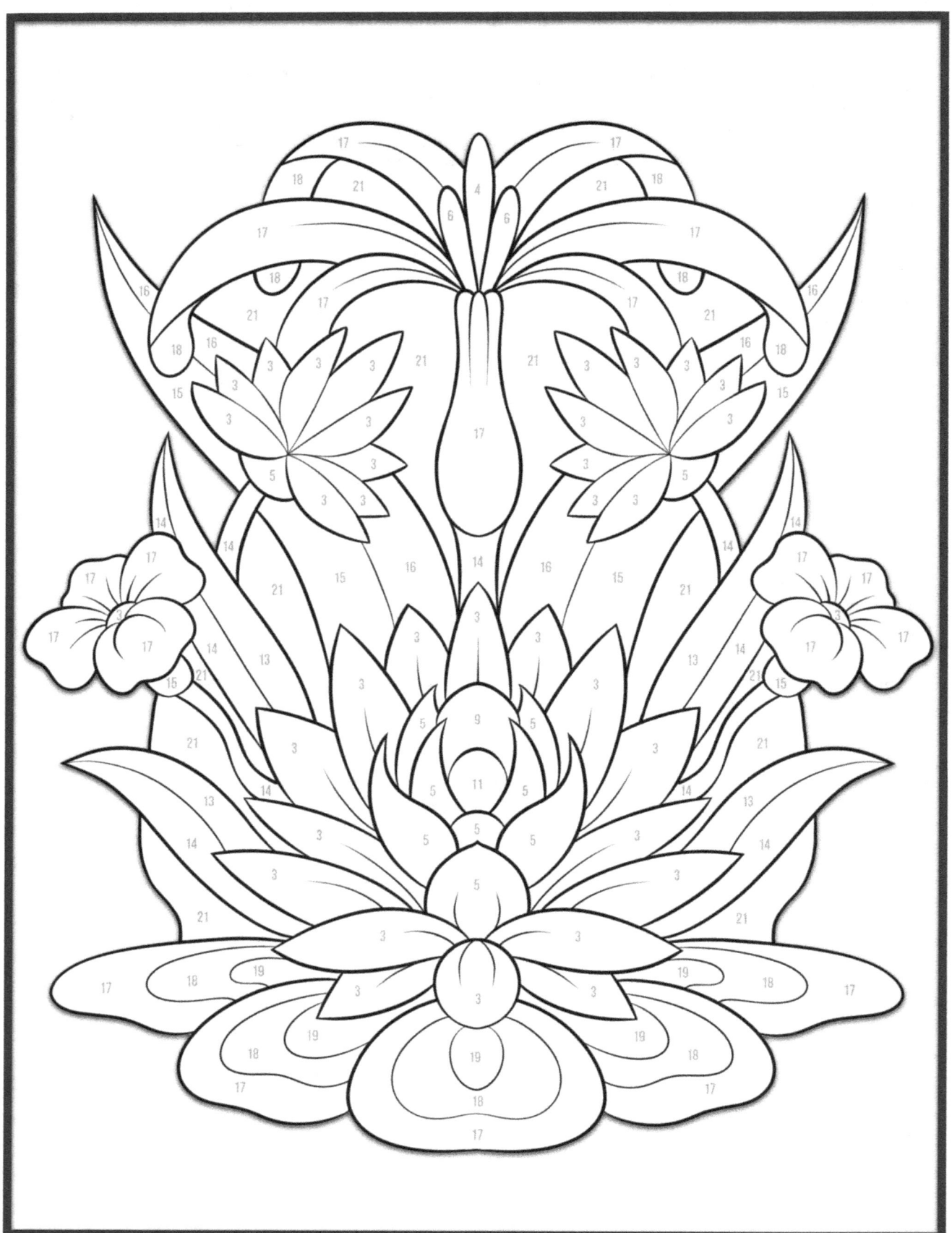

CUSTOM COLOR CHART

☐	1. WHITE	☐	2. LIGHT YELLOW	☐	3. MEDIUM YELLOW
☐	4. DARK YELLOW	☐	5. YELLOW ORANGE	☐	6. LIGHT ORANGE
☐	7. MEDIUM ORANGE	☐	8. DARK ORANGE	☐	9. ORANGE RED
☐	10. PINK	☐	11. MEDIUM RED	☐	12. DARK RED
☐	13. LIGHT GREEN	☐	14. MEDIUM GREEN	☐	15. DARK GREEN
☐	16. GREEN BLUE	☐	17. LIGHT BLUE	☐	18. MEDIUM BLUE
☐	19. DARK BLUE	☐	20. BLUE PURPLE	☐	21. LIGHT PURPLE
☐	22. MEDIUM PURPLE	☐	23. DARK PURPLE	☐	24. LIGHT BROWN
☐	25. MEDIUM BROWN	☐	26. DARK BROWN	☐	27. LIGHT GRAY
☐	28. MEDIUM GRAY	☐	29. DARK GRAY	☐	30. BLACK

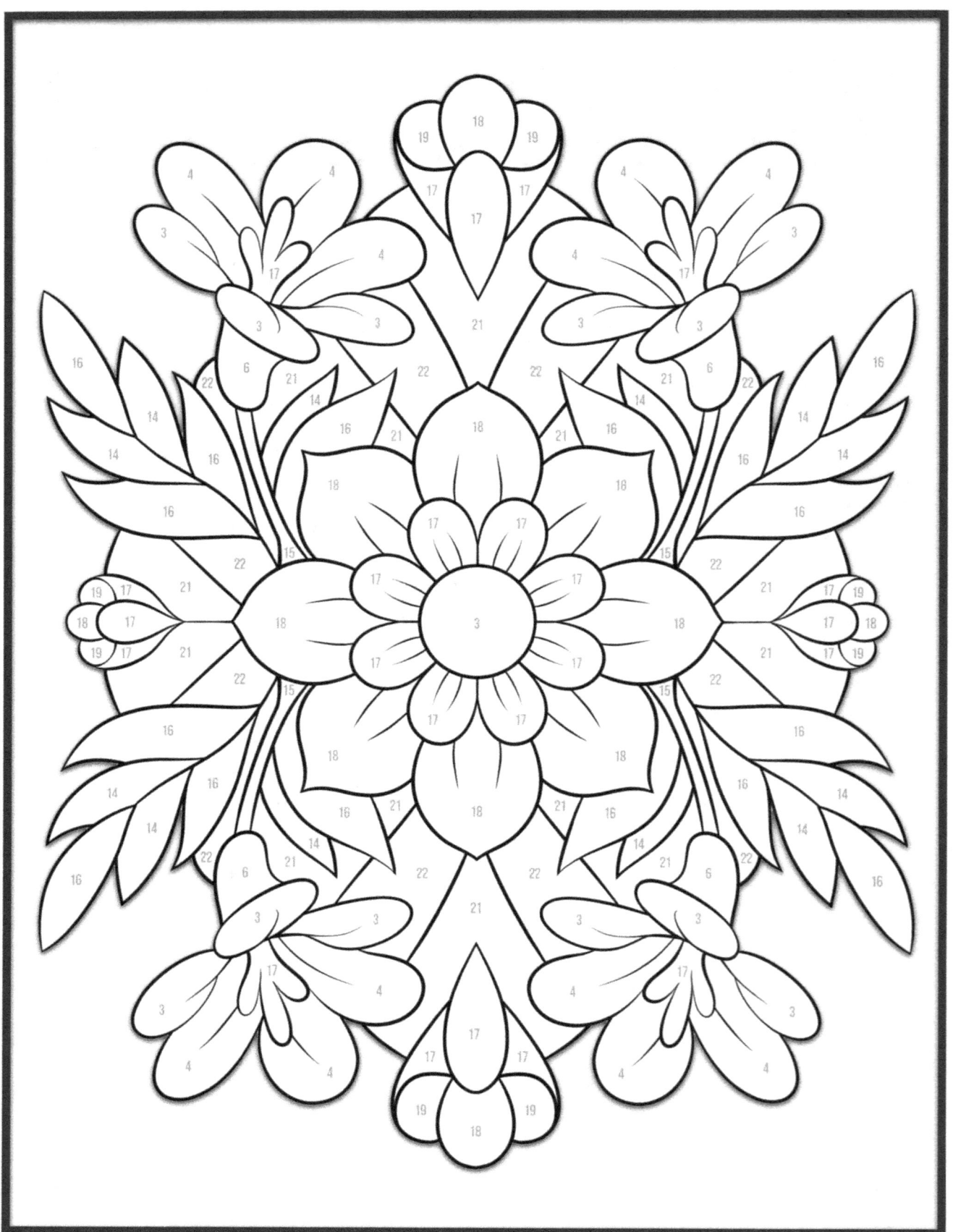

CUSTOM COLOR CHART

1. WHITE
_____

2. LIGHT YELLOW
_____

3. MEDIUM YELLOW
_____

4. DARK YELLOW
_____

5. YELLOW ORANGE
_____

6. LIGHT ORANGE
_____

7. MEDIUM ORANGE
_____

8. DARK ORANGE
_____

9. ORANGE RED
_____

10. PINK
_____

11. MEDIUM RED
_____

12. DARK RED
_____

13. LIGHT GREEN
_____

14. MEDIUM GREEN
_____

15. DARK GREEN
_____

16. GREEN BLUE
_____

17. LIGHT BLUE
_____

18. MEDIUM BLUE
_____

19. DARK BLUE
_____

20. BLUE PURPLE
_____

21. LIGHT PURPLE
_____

22. MEDIUM PURPLE
_____

23. DARK PURPLE
_____

24. LIGHT BROWN
_____

25. MEDIUM BROWN
_____

26. DARK BROWN
_____

27. LIGHT GRAY
_____

28. MEDIUM GRAY
_____

29. DARK GRAY
_____

30. BLACK
_____

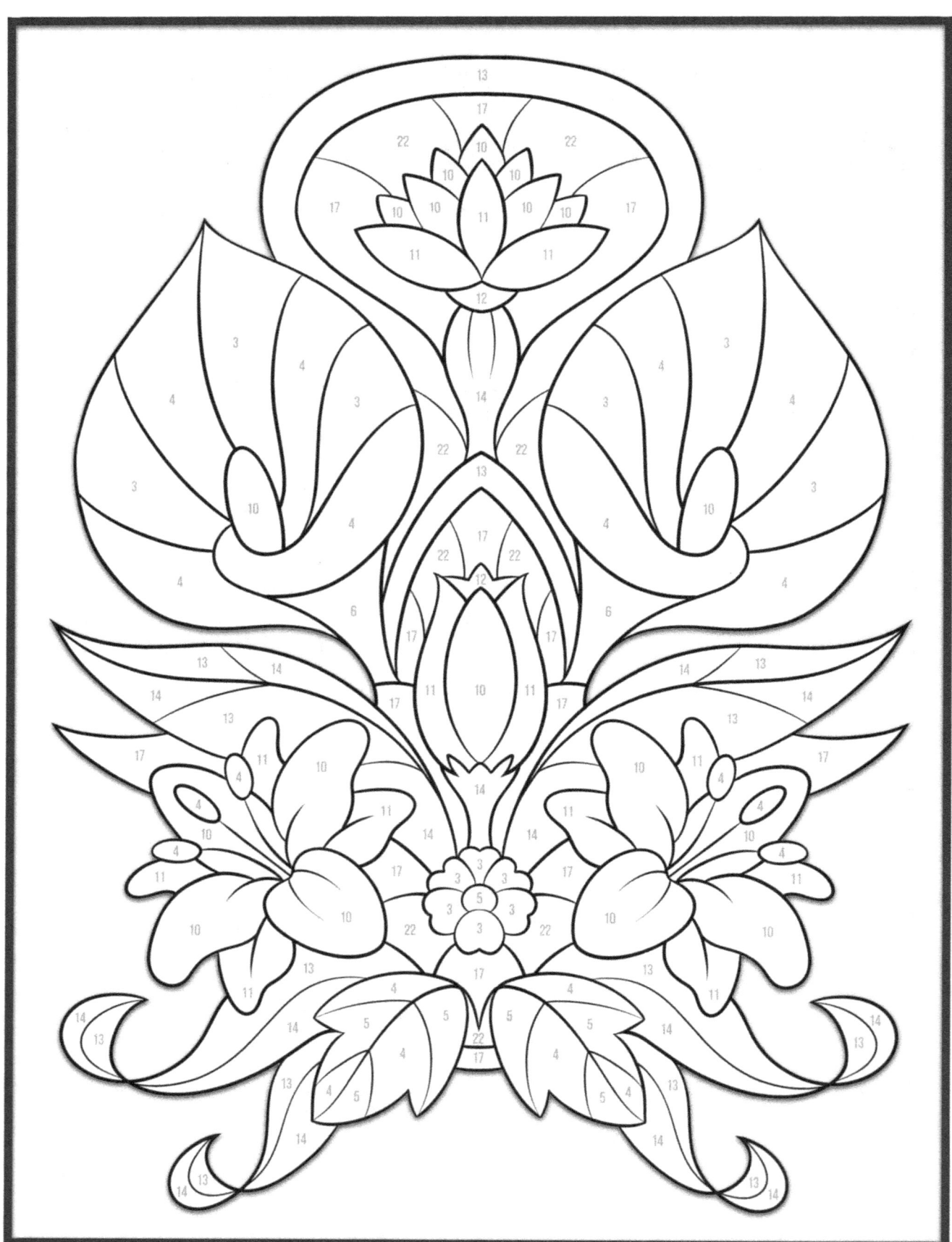

CUSTOM COLOR CHART

☐	1. WHITE	☐	2. LIGHT YELLOW	☐	3. MEDIUM YELLOW
☐	4. DARK YELLOW	☐	5. YELLOW ORANGE	☐	6. LIGHT ORANGE
☐	7. MEDIUM ORANGE	☐	8. DARK ORANGE	☐	9. ORANGE RED
☐	10. PINK	☐	11. MEDIUM RED	☐	12. DARK RED
☐	13. LIGHT GREEN	☐	14. MEDIUM GREEN	☐	15. DARK GREEN
☐	16. GREEN BLUE	☐	17. LIGHT BLUE	☐	18. MEDIUM BLUE
☐	19. DARK BLUE	☐	20. BLUE PURPLE	☐	21. LIGHT PURPLE
☐	22. MEDIUM PURPLE	☐	23. DARK PURPLE	☐	24. LIGHT BROWN
☐	25. MEDIUM BROWN	☐	26. DARK BROWN	☐	27. LIGHT GRAY
☐	28. MEDIUM GRAY	☐	29. DARK GRAY	☐	30. BLACK

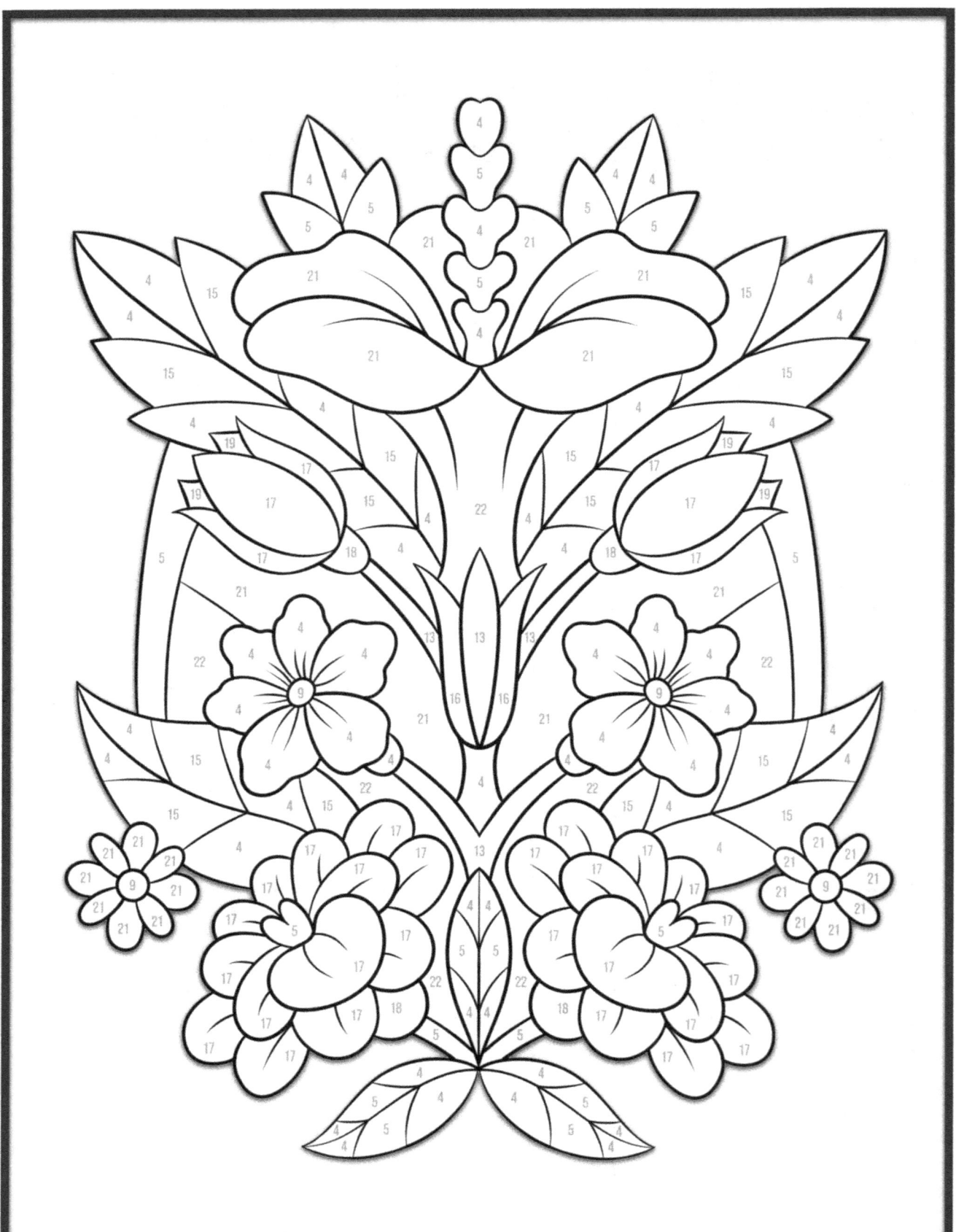

CUSTOM COLOR CHART

1. WHITE
_____

2. LIGHT YELLOW
_____

3. MEDIUM YELLOW
_____

4. DARK YELLOW
_____

5. YELLOW ORANGE
_____

6. LIGHT ORANGE
_____

7. MEDIUM ORANGE
_____

8. DARK ORANGE
_____

9. ORANGE RED
_____

10. PINK
_____

11. MEDIUM RED
_____

12. DARK RED
_____

13. LIGHT GREEN
_____

14. MEDIUM GREEN
_____

15. DARK GREEN
_____

16. GREEN BLUE
_____

17. LIGHT BLUE
_____

18. MEDIUM BLUE
_____

19. DARK BLUE
_____

20. BLUE PURPLE
_____

21. LIGHT PURPLE
_____

22. MEDIUM PURPLE
_____

23. DARK PURPLE
_____

24. LIGHT BROWN
_____

25. MEDIUM BROWN
_____

26. DARK BROWN
_____

27. LIGHT GRAY
_____

28. MEDIUM GRAY
_____

29. DARK GRAY
_____

30. BLACK
_____

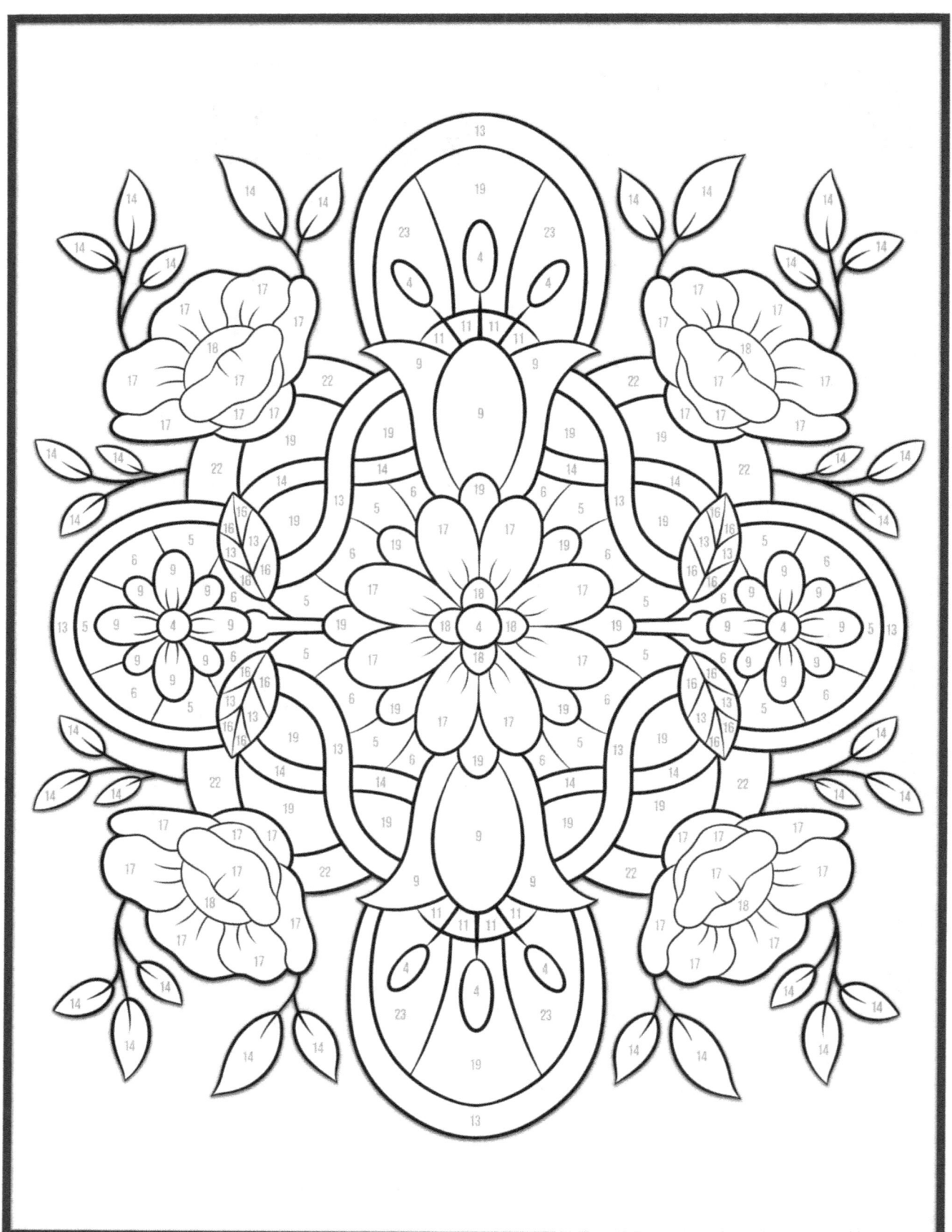

CUSTOM COLOR CHART

☐	1. WHITE	☐	2. LIGHT YELLOW	☐	3. MEDIUM YELLOW
☐	4. DARK YELLOW	☐	5. YELLOW ORANGE	☐	6. LIGHT ORANGE
☐	7. MEDIUM ORANGE	☐	8. DARK ORANGE	☐	9. ORANGE RED
☐	10. PINK	☐	11. MEDIUM RED	☐	12. DARK RED
☐	13. LIGHT GREEN	☐	14. MEDIUM GREEN	☐	15. DARK GREEN
☐	16. GREEN BLUE	☐	17. LIGHT BLUE	☐	18. MEDIUM BLUE
☐	19. DARK BLUE	☐	20. BLUE PURPLE	☐	21. LIGHT PURPLE
☐	22. MEDIUM PURPLE	☐	23. DARK PURPLE	☐	24. LIGHT BROWN
☐	25. MEDIUM BROWN	☐	26. DARK BROWN	☐	27. LIGHT GRAY
☐	28. MEDIUM GRAY	☐	29. DARK GRAY	☐	30. BLACK

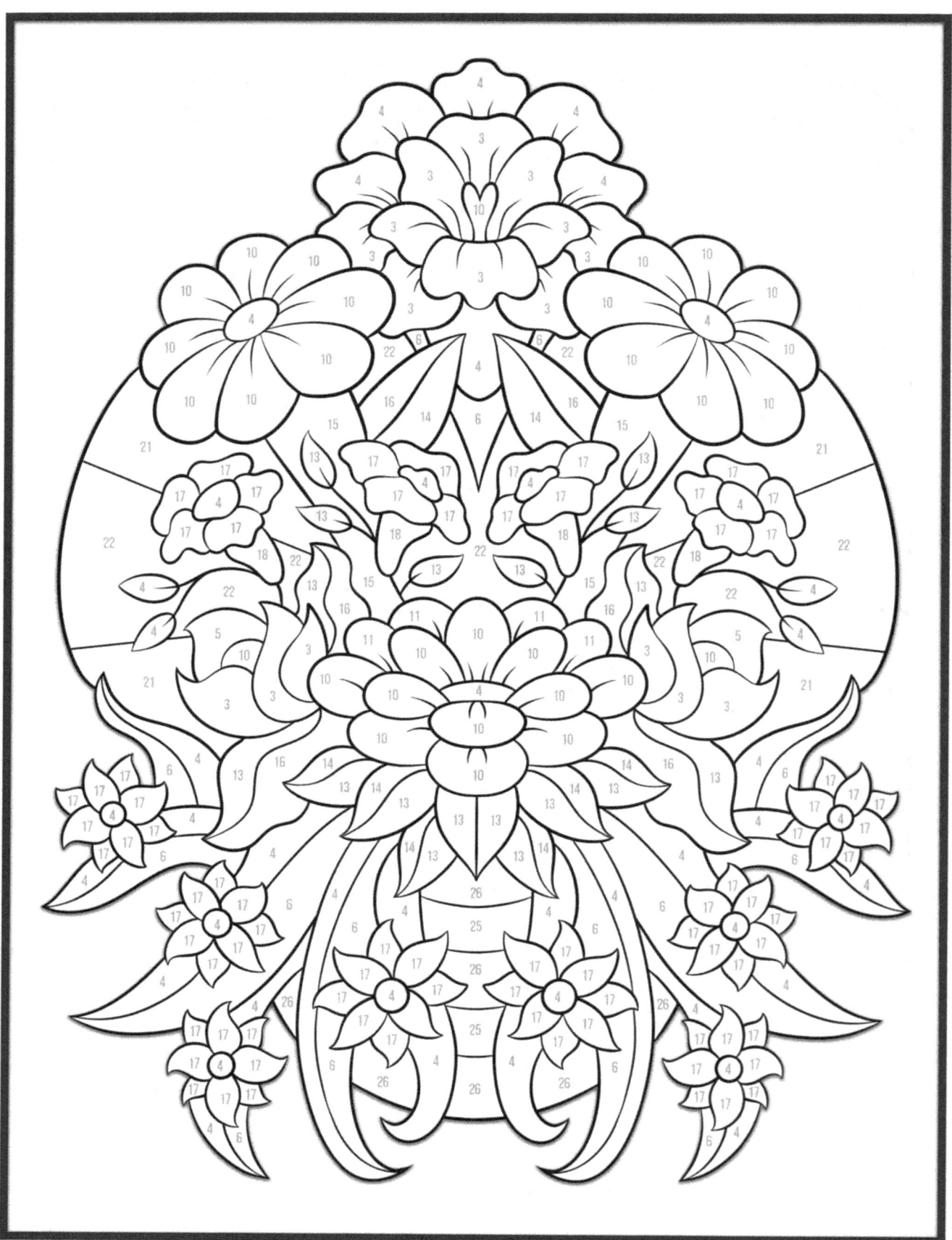

CUSTOM COLOR CHART

1. WHITE	2. LIGHT YELLOW	3. MEDIUM YELLOW
4. DARK YELLOW	5. YELLOW ORANGE	6. LIGHT ORANGE
7. MEDIUM ORANGE	8. DARK ORANGE	9. ORANGE RED
10. PINK	11. MEDIUM RED	12. DARK RED
13. LIGHT GREEN	14. MEDIUM GREEN	15. DARK GREEN
16. GREEN BLUE	17. LIGHT BLUE	18. MEDIUM BLUE
19. DARK BLUE	20. BLUE PURPLE	21. LIGHT PURPLE
22. MEDIUM PURPLE	23. DARK PURPLE	24. LIGHT BROWN
25. MEDIUM BROWN	26. DARK BROWN	27. LIGHT GRAY
28. MEDIUM GRAY	29. DARK GRAY	30. BLACK

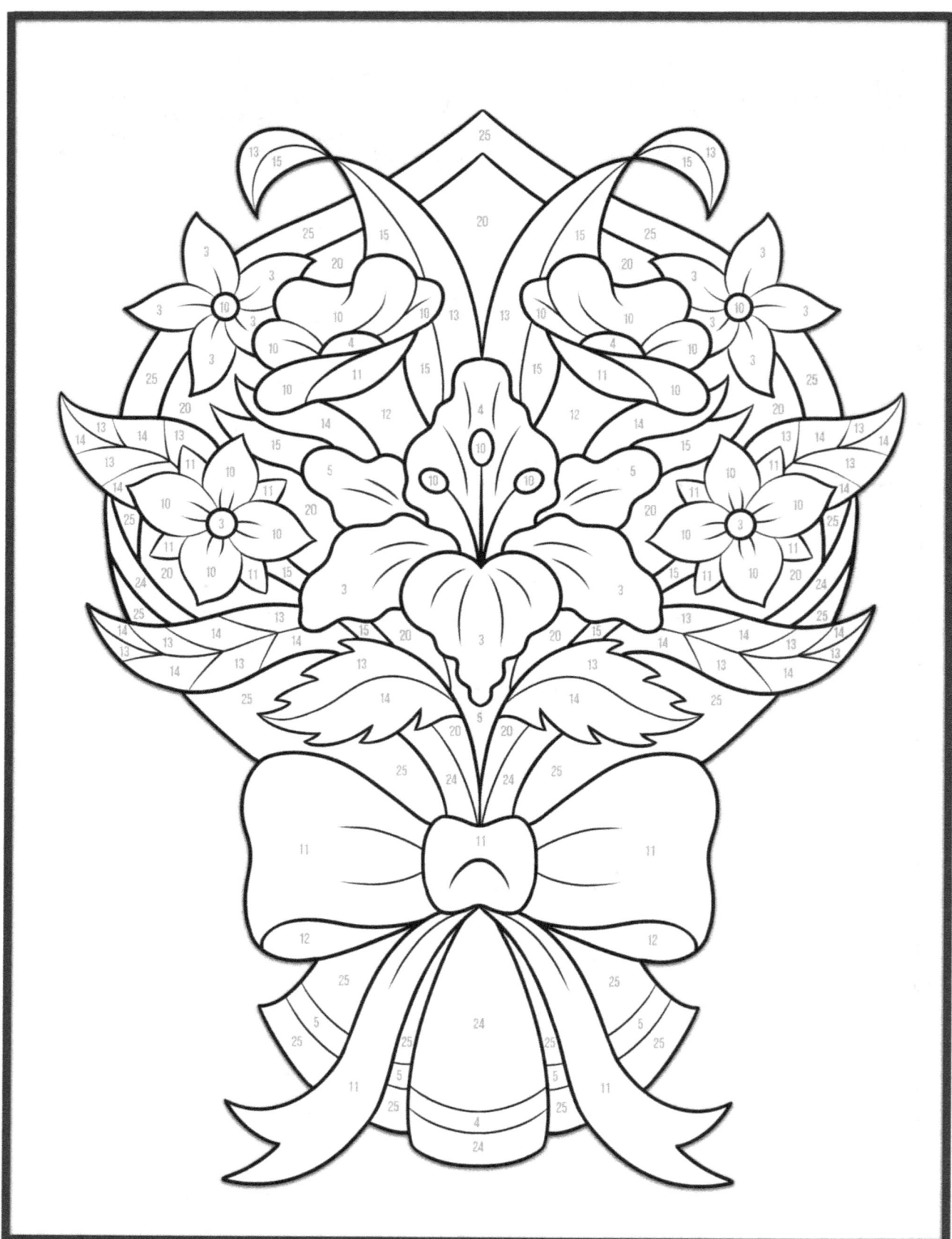

CUSTOM COLOR CHART

1. WHITE	2. LIGHT YELLOW	3. MEDIUM YELLOW
4. DARK YELLOW	5. YELLOW ORANGE	6. LIGHT ORANGE
7. MEDIUM ORANGE	8. DARK ORANGE	9. ORANGE RED
10. PINK	11. MEDIUM RED	12. DARK RED
13. LIGHT GREEN	14. MEDIUM GREEN	15. DARK GREEN
16. GREEN BLUE	17. LIGHT BLUE	18. MEDIUM BLUE
19. DARK BLUE	20. BLUE PURPLE	21. LIGHT PURPLE
22. MEDIUM PURPLE	23. DARK PURPLE	24. LIGHT BROWN
25. MEDIUM BROWN	26. DARK BROWN	27. LIGHT GRAY
28. MEDIUM GRAY	29. DARK GRAY	30. BLACK

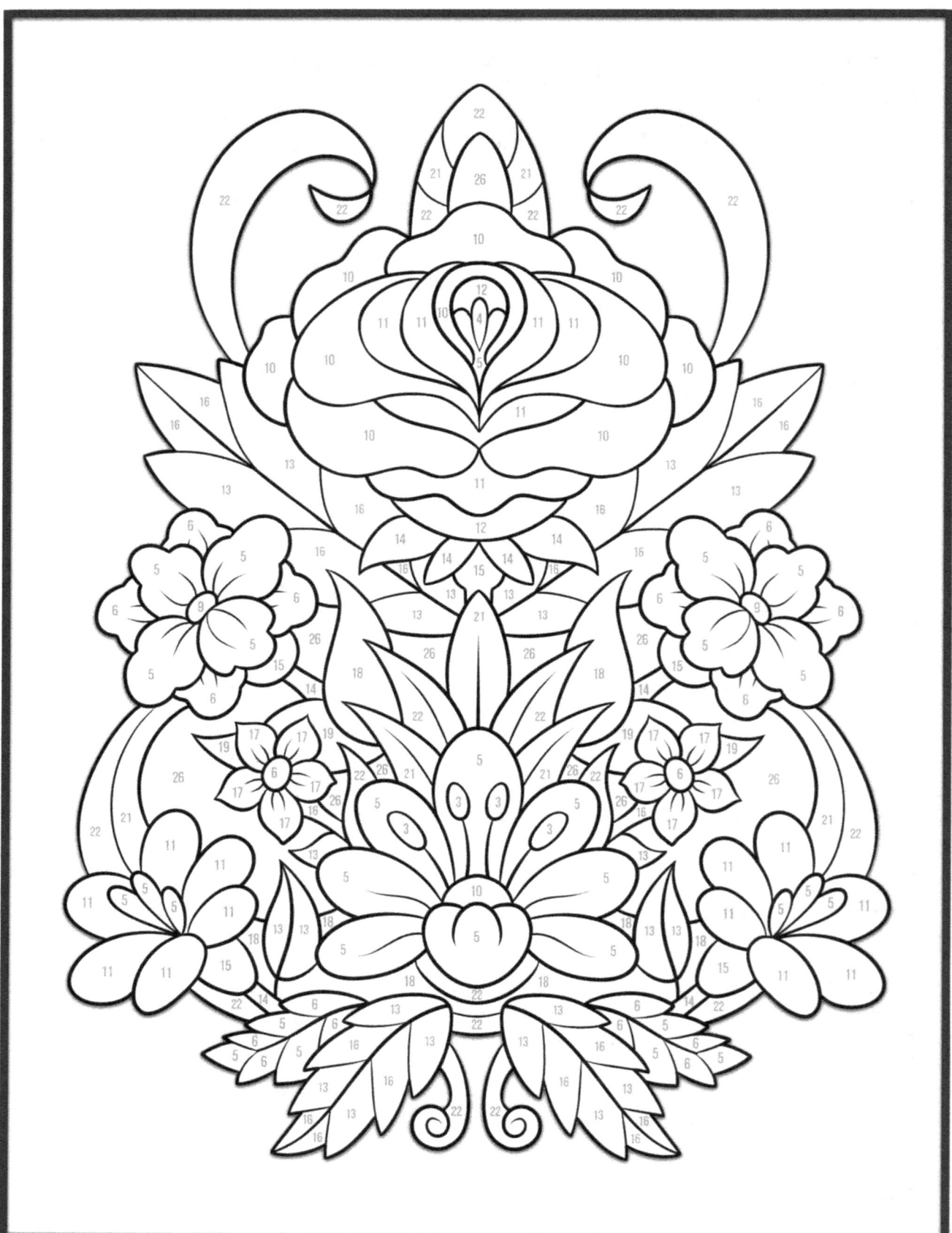

CUSTOM COLOR CHART

1. WHITE
_____

2. LIGHT YELLOW
_____

3. MEDIUM YELLOW
_____

4. DARK YELLOW
_____

5. YELLOW ORANGE
_____

6. LIGHT ORANGE
_____

7. MEDIUM ORANGE
_____

8. DARK ORANGE
_____

9. ORANGE RED
_____

10. PINK
_____

11. MEDIUM RED
_____

12. DARK RED
_____

13. LIGHT GREEN
_____

14. MEDIUM GREEN
_____

15. DARK GREEN
_____

16. GREEN BLUE
_____

17. LIGHT BLUE
_____

18. MEDIUM BLUE
_____

19. DARK BLUE
_____

20. BLUE PURPLE
_____

21. LIGHT PURPLE
_____

22. MEDIUM PURPLE
_____

23. DARK PURPLE
_____

24. LIGHT BROWN
_____

25. MEDIUM BROWN
_____

26. DARK BROWN
_____

27. LIGHT GRAY
_____

28. MEDIUM GRAY
_____

29. DARK GRAY
_____

30. BLACK
_____

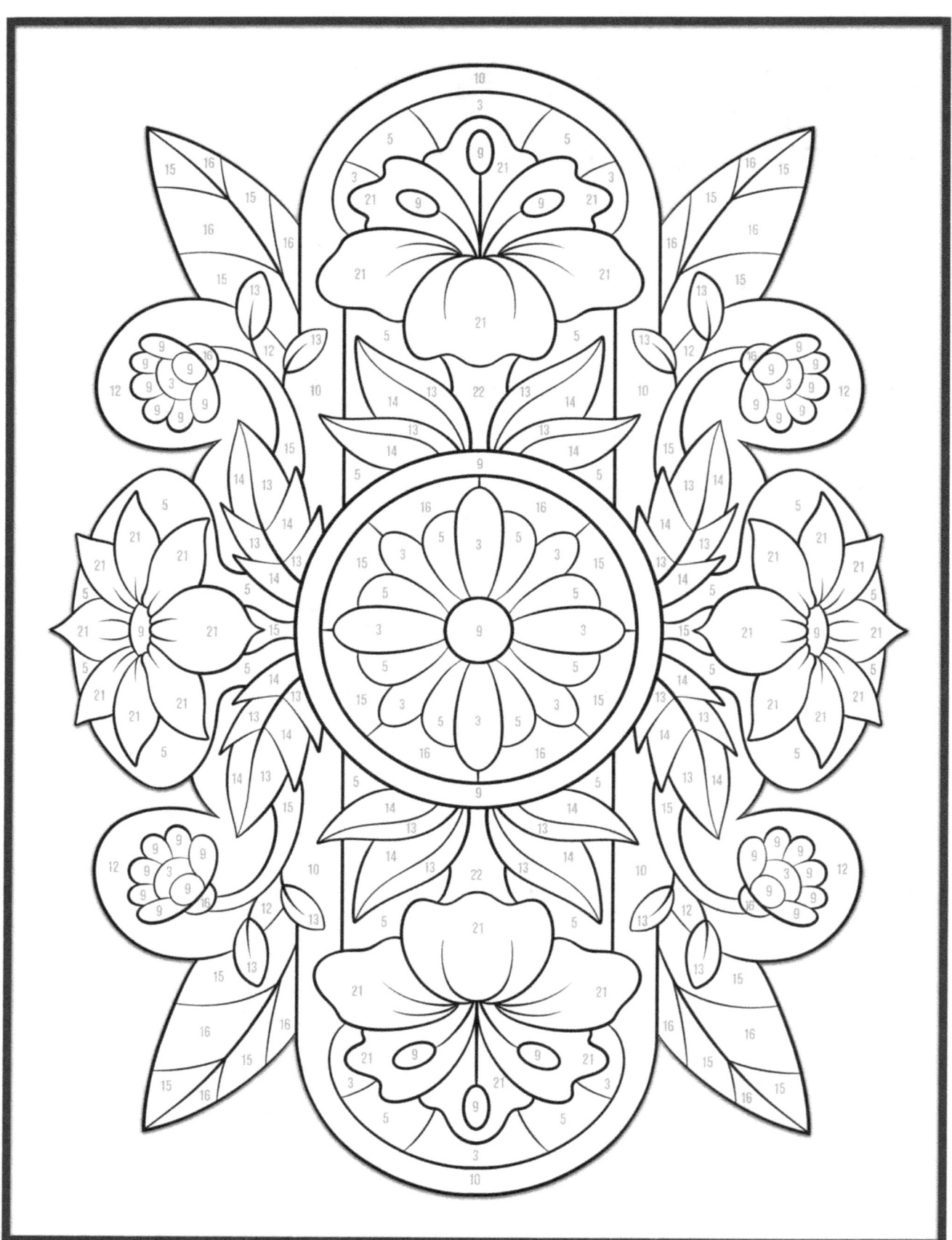

CUSTOM COLOR CHART

1. WHITE
_____

2. LIGHT YELLOW
_____

3. MEDIUM YELLOW
_____

4. DARK YELLOW
_____

5. YELLOW ORANGE
_____

6. LIGHT ORANGE
_____

7. MEDIUM ORANGE
_____

8. DARK ORANGE
_____

9. ORANGE RED
_____

10. PINK
_____

11. MEDIUM RED
_____

12. DARK RED
_____

13. LIGHT GREEN
_____

14. MEDIUM GREEN
_____

15. DARK GREEN
_____

16. GREEN BLUE
_____

17. LIGHT BLUE
_____

18. MEDIUM BLUE
_____

19. DARK BLUE
_____

20. BLUE PURPLE
_____

21. LIGHT PURPLE
_____

22. MEDIUM PURPLE
_____

23. DARK PURPLE
_____

24. LIGHT BROWN
_____

25. MEDIUM BROWN
_____

26. DARK BROWN
_____

27. LIGHT GRAY
_____

28. MEDIUM GRAY
_____

29. DARK GRAY
_____

30. BLACK
_____

CUSTOM COLOR CHART

☐	1. WHITE	☐	2. LIGHT YELLOW	☐	3. MEDIUM YELLOW
☐	4. DARK YELLOW	☐	5. YELLOW ORANGE	☐	6. LIGHT ORANGE
☐	7. MEDIUM ORANGE	☐	8. DARK ORANGE	☐	9. ORANGE RED
☐	10. PINK	☐	11. MEDIUM RED	☐	12. DARK RED
☐	13. LIGHT GREEN	☐	14. MEDIUM GREEN	☐	15. DARK GREEN
☐	16. GREEN BLUE	☐	17. LIGHT BLUE	☐	18. MEDIUM BLUE
☐	19. DARK BLUE	☐	20. BLUE PURPLE	☐	21. LIGHT PURPLE
☐	22. MEDIUM PURPLE	☐	23. DARK PURPLE	☐	24. LIGHT BROWN
☐	25. MEDIUM BROWN	☐	26. DARK BROWN	☐	27. LIGHT GRAY
☐	28. MEDIUM GRAY	☐	29. DARK GRAY	☐	30. BLACK

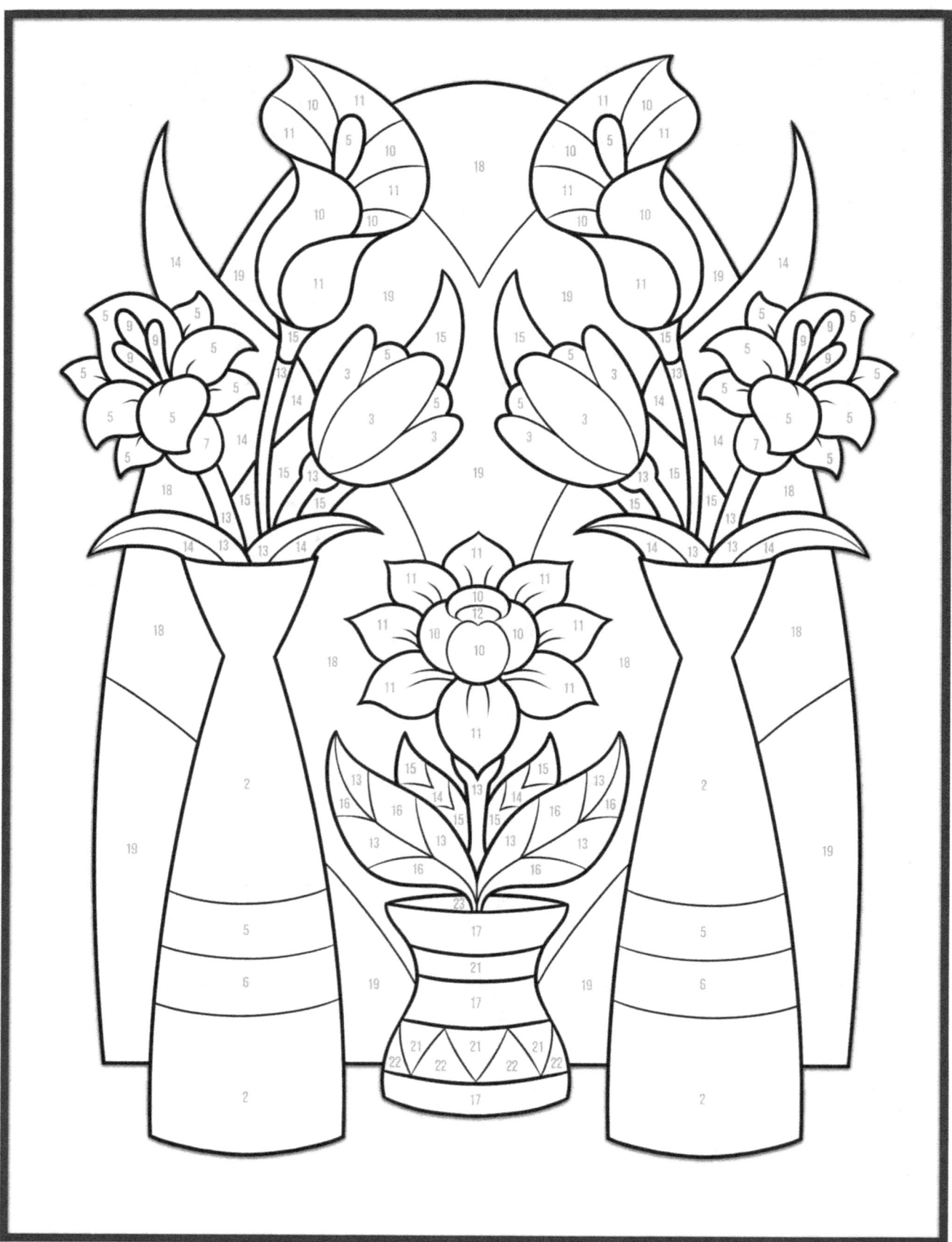

CUSTOM COLOR CHART

1. WHITE _____

2. LIGHT YELLOW _____

3. MEDIUM YELLOW _____

4. DARK YELLOW _____

5. YELLOW ORANGE _____

6. LIGHT ORANGE _____

7. MEDIUM ORANGE _____

8. DARK ORANGE _____

9. ORANGE RED _____

10. PINK _____

11. MEDIUM RED _____

12. DARK RED _____

13. LIGHT GREEN _____

14. MEDIUM GREEN _____

15. DARK GREEN _____

16. GREEN BLUE _____

17. LIGHT BLUE _____

18. MEDIUM BLUE _____

19. DARK BLUE _____

20. BLUE PURPLE _____

21. LIGHT PURPLE _____

22. MEDIUM PURPLE _____

23. DARK PURPLE _____

24. LIGHT BROWN _____

25. MEDIUM BROWN _____

26. DARK BROWN _____

27. LIGHT GRAY _____

28. MEDIUM GRAY _____

29. DARK GRAY _____

30. BLACK _____

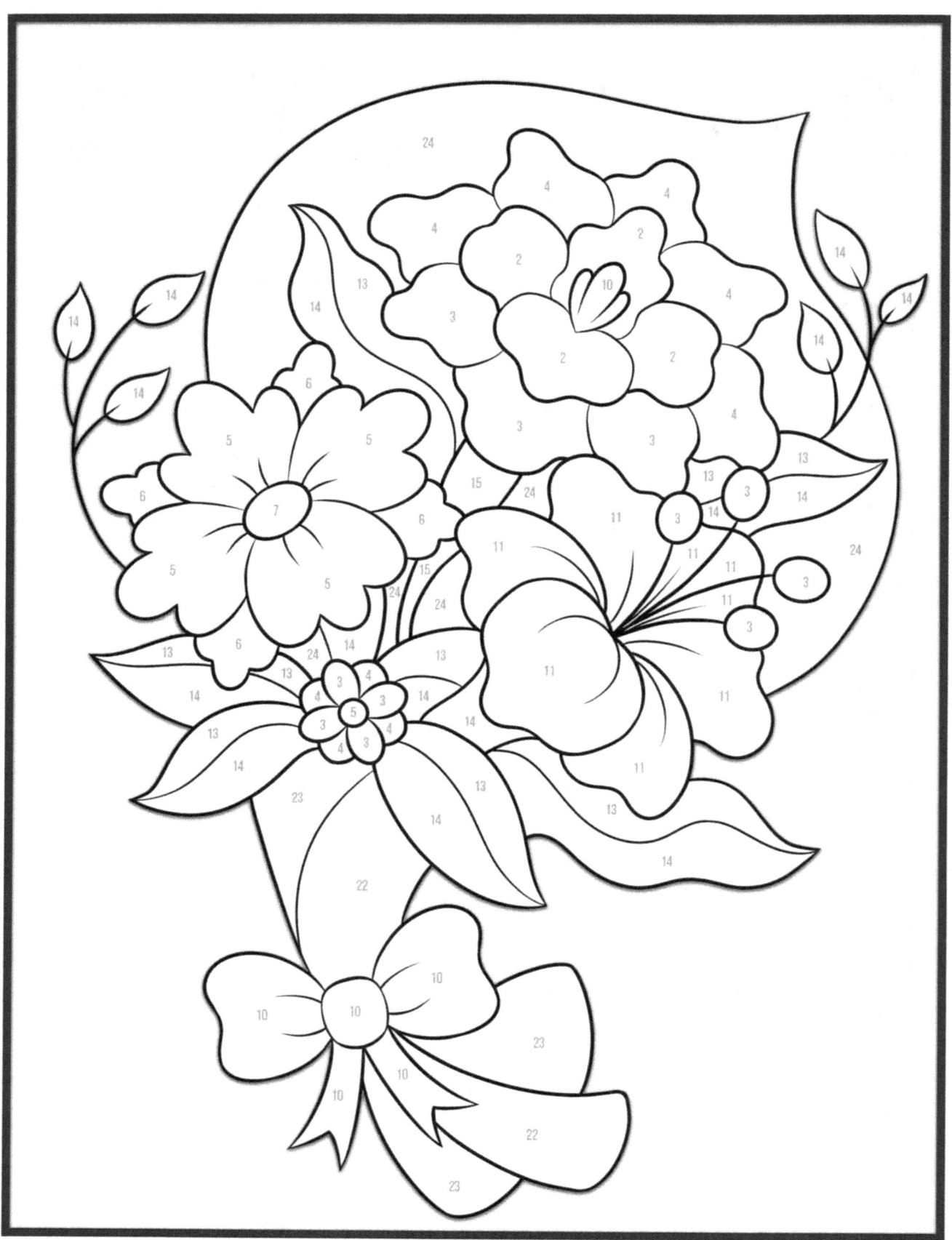

CUSTOM COLOR CHART

☐ 1. WHITE	☐ 2. LIGHT YELLOW	☐ 3. MEDIUM YELLOW
☐ 4. DARK YELLOW	☐ 5. YELLOW ORANGE	☐ 6. LIGHT ORANGE
☐ 7. MEDIUM ORANGE	☐ 8. DARK ORANGE	☐ 9. ORANGE RED
☐ 10. PINK	☐ 11. MEDIUM RED	☐ 12. DARK RED
☐ 13. LIGHT GREEN	☐ 14. MEDIUM GREEN	☐ 15. DARK GREEN
☐ 16. GREEN BLUE	☐ 17. LIGHT BLUE	☐ 18. MEDIUM BLUE
☐ 19. DARK BLUE	☐ 20. BLUE PURPLE	☐ 21. LIGHT PURPLE
☐ 22. MEDIUM PURPLE	☐ 23. DARK PURPLE	☐ 24. LIGHT BROWN
☐ 25. MEDIUM BROWN	☐ 26. DARK BROWN	☐ 27. LIGHT GRAY
☐ 28. MEDIUM GRAY	☐ 29. DARK GRAY	☐ 30. BLACK

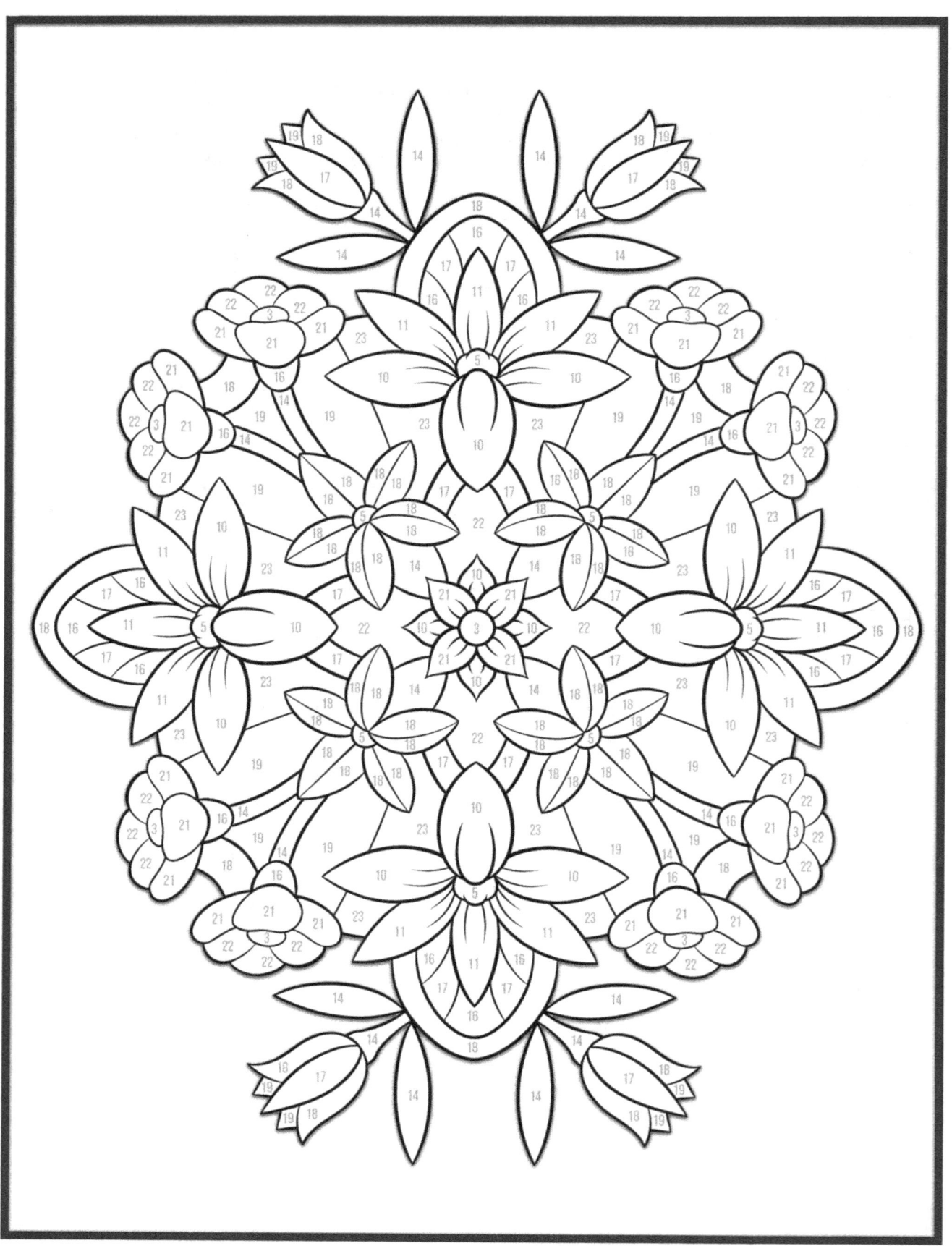

CUSTOM COLOR CHART

1. WHITE

2. LIGHT YELLOW

3. MEDIUM YELLOW

4. DARK YELLOW

5. YELLOW ORANGE

6. LIGHT ORANGE

7. MEDIUM ORANGE

8. DARK ORANGE

9. ORANGE RED

10. PINK

11. MEDIUM RED

12. DARK RED

13. LIGHT GREEN

14. MEDIUM GREEN

15. DARK GREEN

16. GREEN BLUE

17. LIGHT BLUE

18. MEDIUM BLUE

19. DARK BLUE

20. BLUE PURPLE

21. LIGHT PURPLE

22. MEDIUM PURPLE

23. DARK PURPLE

24. LIGHT BROWN

25. MEDIUM BROWN

26. DARK BROWN

27. LIGHT GRAY

28. MEDIUM GRAY

29. DARK GRAY

30. BLACK

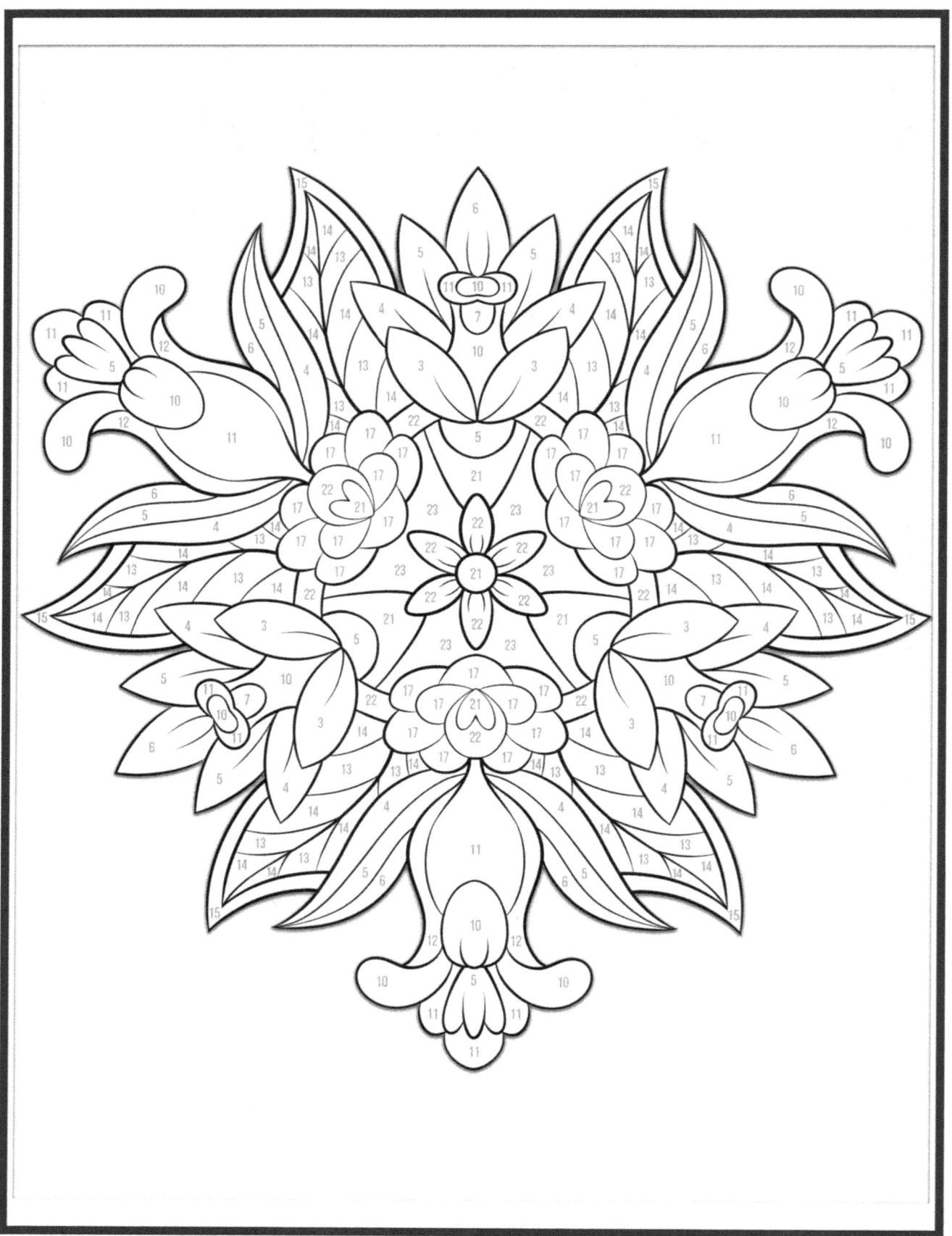

CUSTOM COLOR CHART

1. WHITE
_____

2. LIGHT YELLOW
_____

3. MEDIUM YELLOW
_____

4. DARK YELLOW
_____

5. YELLOW ORANGE
_____

6. LIGHT ORANGE
_____

7. MEDIUM ORANGE
_____

8. DARK ORANGE
_____

9. ORANGE RED
_____

10. PINK
_____

11. MEDIUM RED
_____

12. DARK RED
_____

13. LIGHT GREEN
_____

14. MEDIUM GREEN
_____

15. DARK GREEN
_____

16. GREEN BLUE
_____

17. LIGHT BLUE
_____

18. MEDIUM BLUE
_____

19. DARK BLUE
_____

20. BLUE PURPLE
_____

21. LIGHT PURPLE
_____

22. MEDIUM PURPLE
_____

23. DARK PURPLE
_____

24. LIGHT BROWN
_____

25. MEDIUM BROWN
_____

26. DARK BROWN
_____

27. LIGHT GRAY
_____

28. MEDIUM GRAY
_____

29. DARK GRAY
_____

30. BLACK
_____

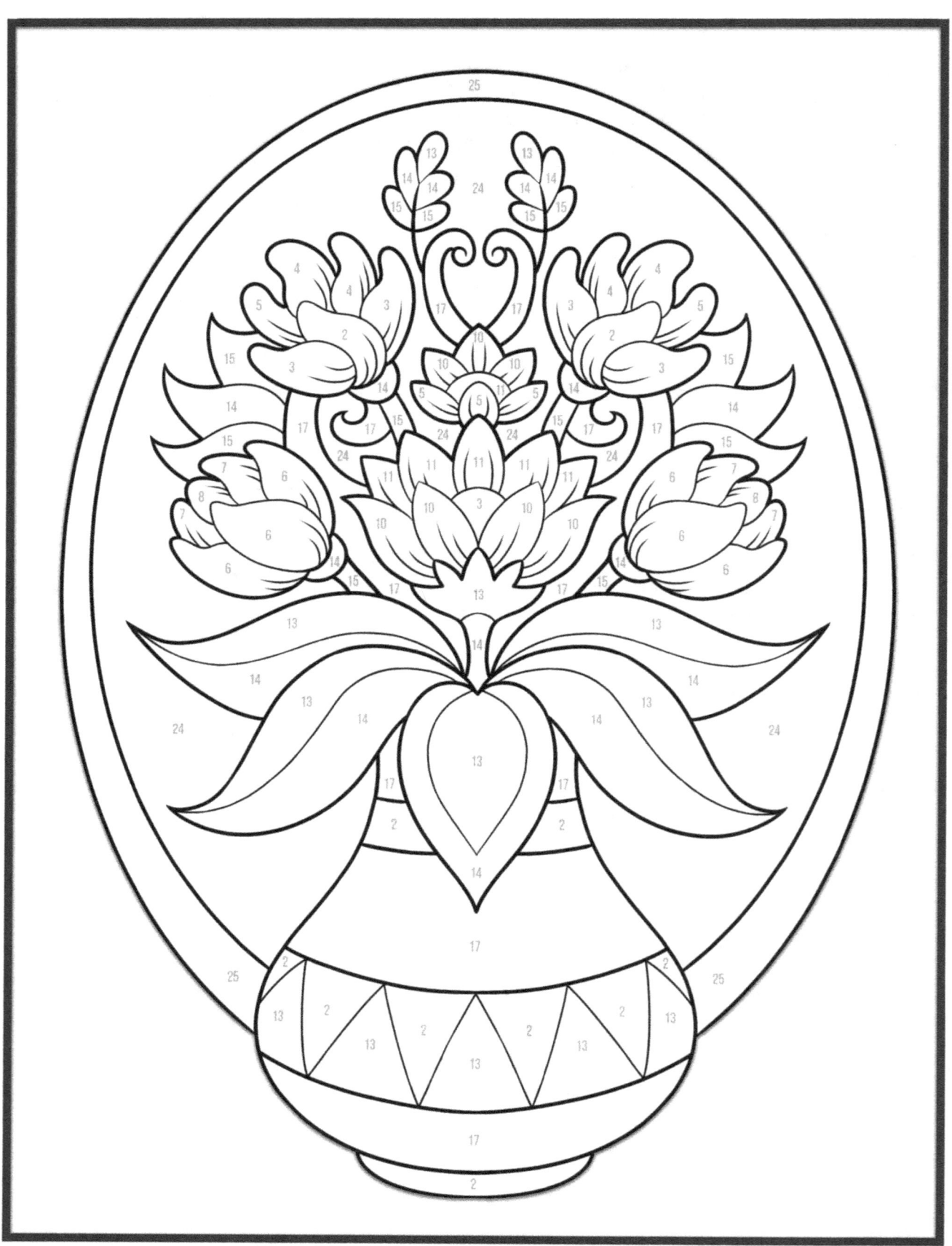

CUSTOM COLOR CHART

1. WHITE

2. LIGHT YELLOW

3. MEDIUM YELLOW

4. DARK YELLOW

5. YELLOW ORANGE

6. LIGHT ORANGE

7. MEDIUM ORANGE

8. DARK ORANGE

9. ORANGE RED

10. PINK

11. MEDIUM RED

12. DARK RED

13. LIGHT GREEN

14. MEDIUM GREEN

15. DARK GREEN

16. GREEN BLUE

17. LIGHT BLUE

18. MEDIUM BLUE

19. DARK BLUE

20. BLUE PURPLE

21. LIGHT PURPLE

22. MEDIUM PURPLE

23. DARK PURPLE

24. LIGHT BROWN

25. MEDIUM BROWN

26. DARK BROWN

27. LIGHT GRAY

28. MEDIUM GRAY

29. DARK GRAY

30. BLACK

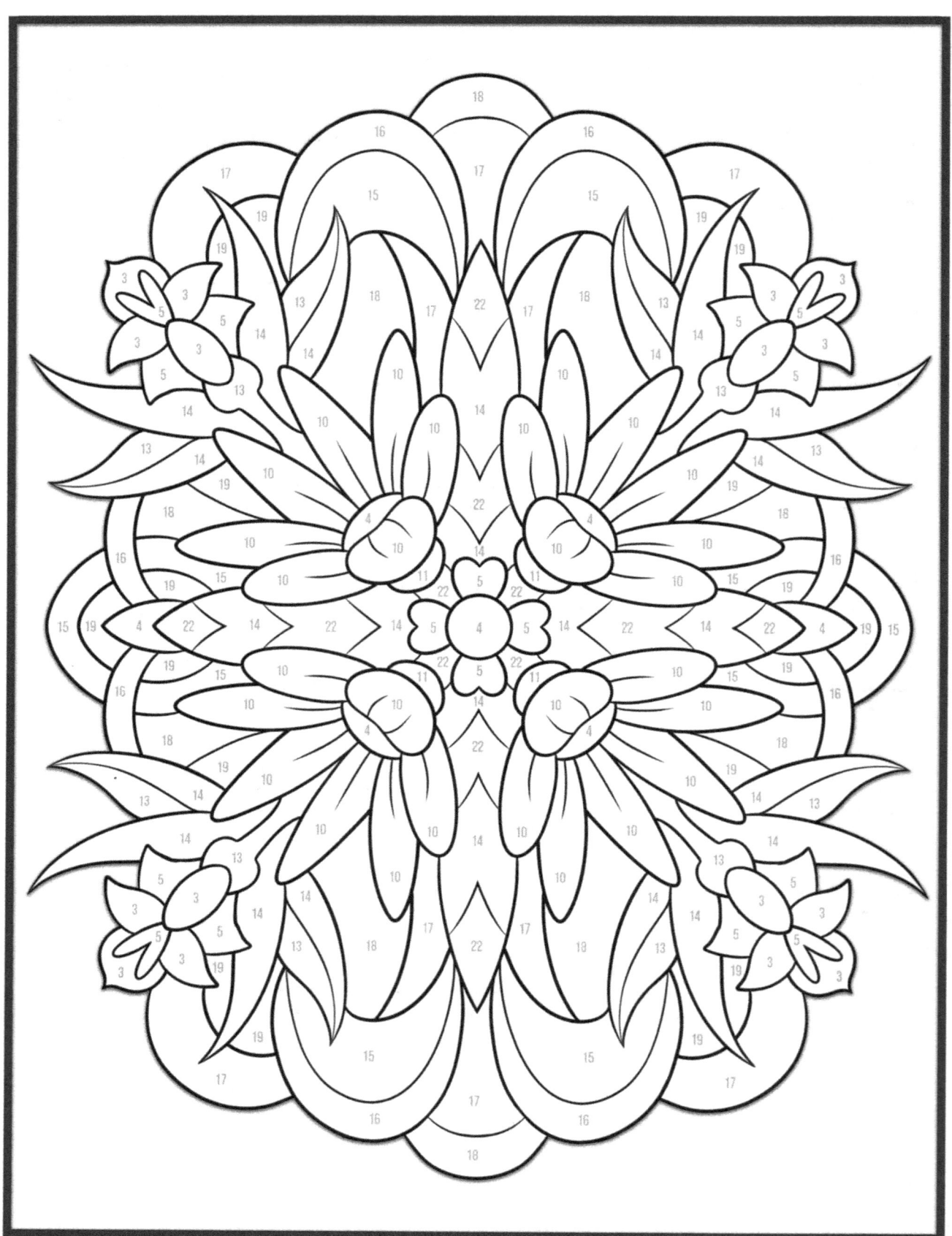

CUSTOM COLOR CHART

1. WHITE

2. LIGHT YELLOW

3. MEDIUM YELLOW

4. DARK YELLOW

5. YELLOW ORANGE

6. LIGHT ORANGE

7. MEDIUM ORANGE

8. DARK ORANGE

9. ORANGE RED

10. PINK

11. MEDIUM RED

12. DARK RED

13. LIGHT GREEN

14. MEDIUM GREEN

15. DARK GREEN

16. GREEN BLUE

17. LIGHT BLUE

18. MEDIUM BLUE

19. DARK BLUE

20. BLUE PURPLE

21. LIGHT PURPLE

22. MEDIUM PURPLE

23. DARK PURPLE

24. LIGHT BROWN

25. MEDIUM BROWN

26. DARK BROWN

27. LIGHT GRAY

28. MEDIUM GRAY

29. DARK GRAY

30. BLACK

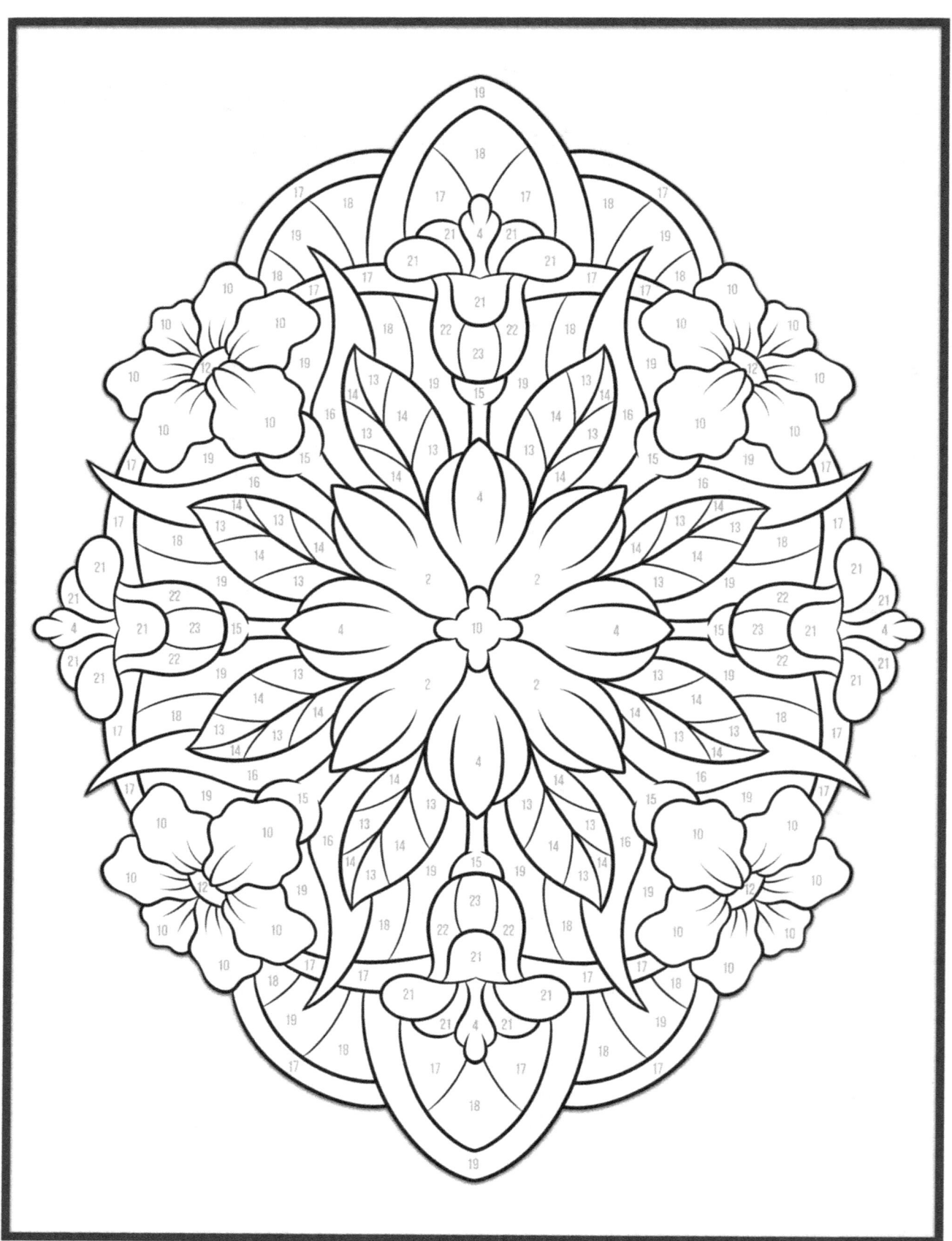

CUSTOM COLOR CHART

1. WHITE
_____

2. LIGHT YELLOW
_____

3. MEDIUM YELLOW
_____

4. DARK YELLOW
_____

5. YELLOW ORANGE
_____

6. LIGHT ORANGE
_____

7. MEDIUM ORANGE
_____

8. DARK ORANGE
_____

9. ORANGE RED
_____

10. PINK
_____

11. MEDIUM RED
_____

12. DARK RED
_____

13. LIGHT GREEN
_____

14. MEDIUM GREEN
_____

15. DARK GREEN
_____

16. GREEN BLUE
_____

17. LIGHT BLUE
_____

18. MEDIUM BLUE
_____

19. DARK BLUE
_____

20. BLUE PURPLE
_____

21. LIGHT PURPLE
_____

22. MEDIUM PURPLE
_____

23. DARK PURPLE
_____

24. LIGHT BROWN
_____

25. MEDIUM BROWN
_____

26. DARK BROWN
_____

27. LIGHT GRAY
_____

28. MEDIUM GRAY
_____

29. DARK GRAY
_____

30. BLACK
_____

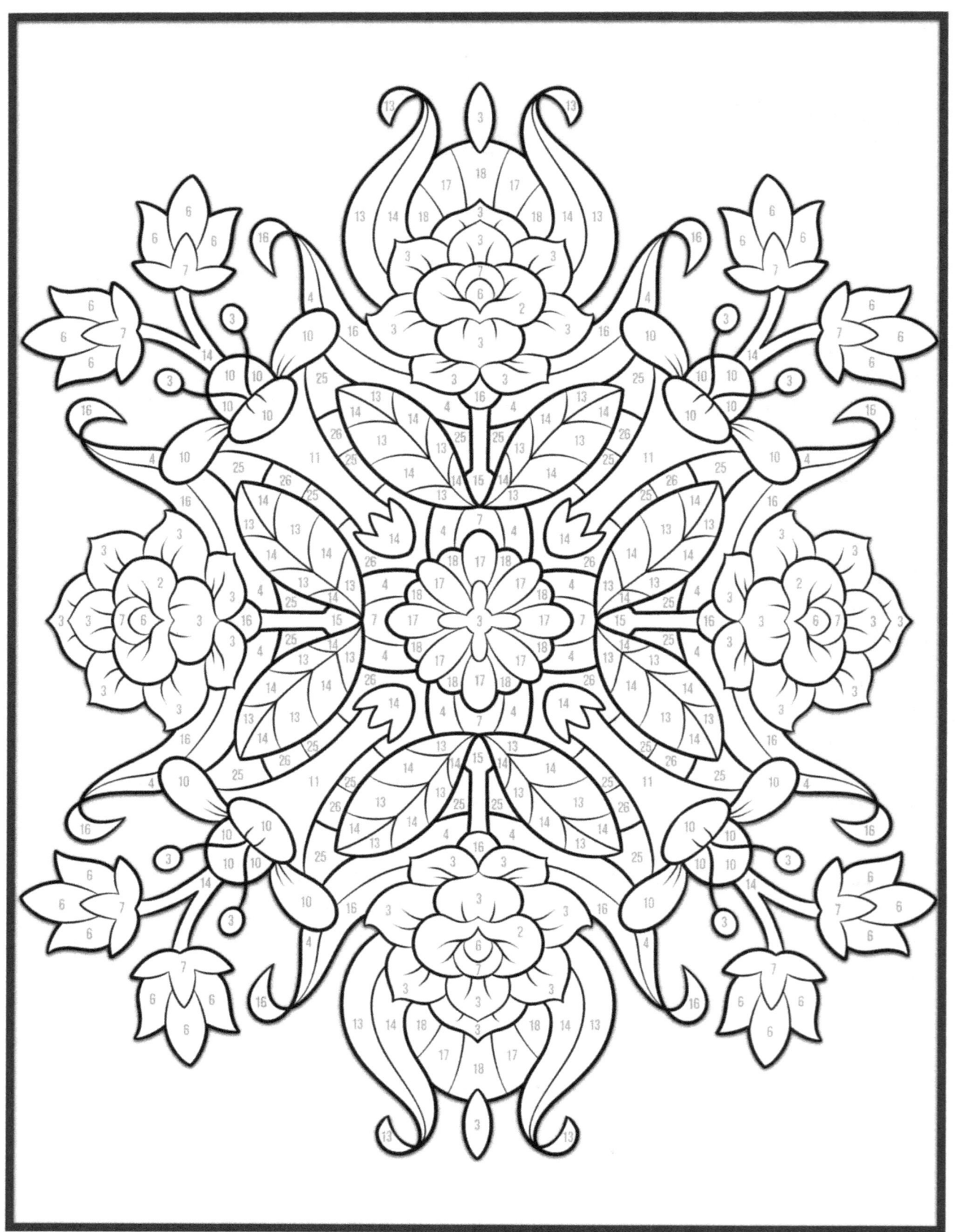

CUSTOM COLOR CHART

1. WHITE

2. LIGHT YELLOW

3. MEDIUM YELLOW

4. DARK YELLOW

5. YELLOW ORANGE

6. LIGHT ORANGE

7. MEDIUM ORANGE

8. DARK ORANGE

9. ORANGE RED

10. PINK

11. MEDIUM RED

12. DARK RED

13. LIGHT GREEN

14. MEDIUM GREEN

15. DARK GREEN

16. GREEN BLUE

17. LIGHT BLUE

18. MEDIUM BLUE

19. DARK BLUE

20. BLUE PURPLE

21. LIGHT PURPLE

22. MEDIUM PURPLE

23. DARK PURPLE

24. LIGHT BROWN

25. MEDIUM BROWN

26. DARK BROWN

27. LIGHT GRAY

28. MEDIUM GRAY

29. DARK GRAY

30. BLACK

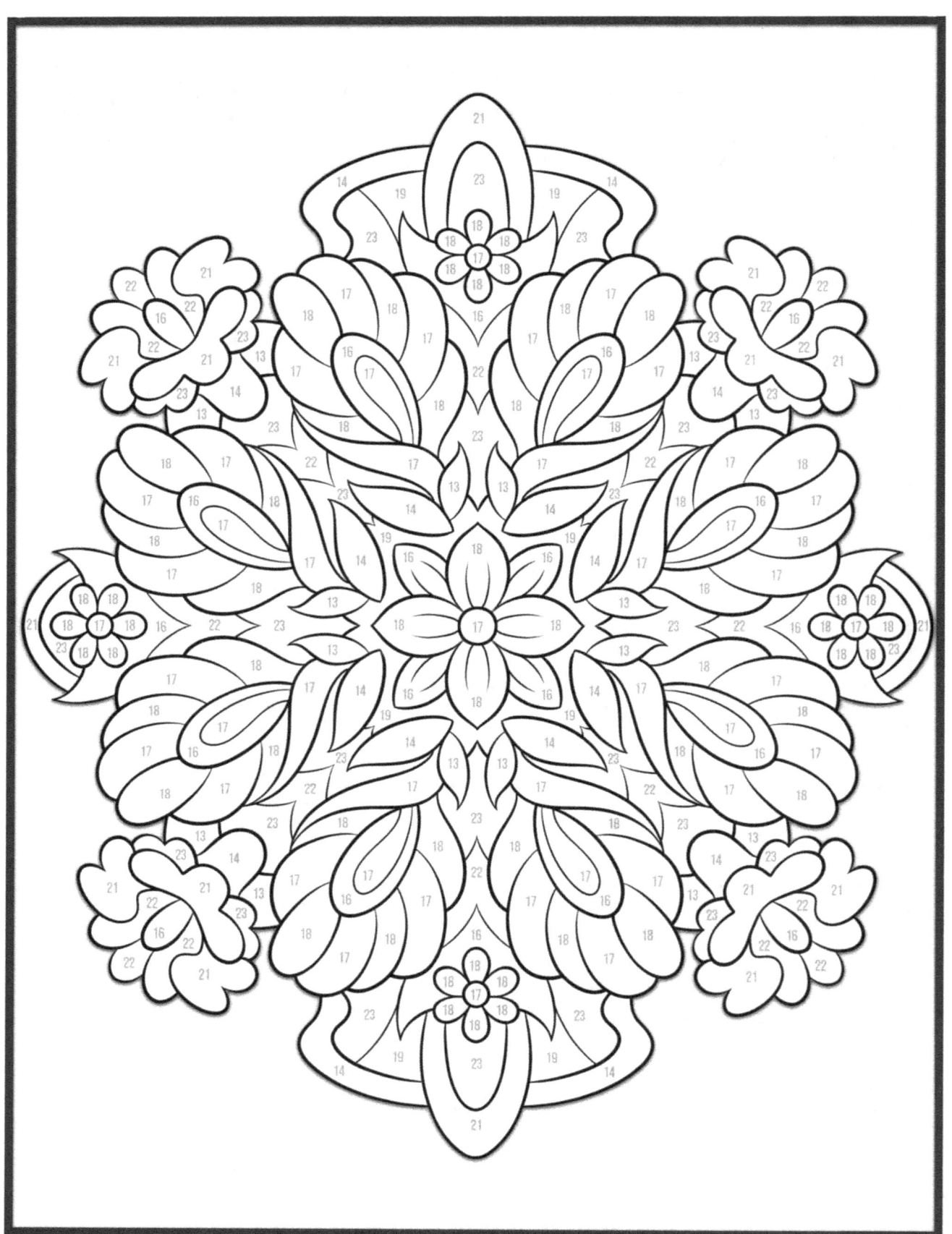

CUSTOM COLOR CHART

	1. WHITE		2. LIGHT YELLOW		3. MEDIUM YELLOW
☐	_____	☐	_____	☐	_____
☐	4. DARK YELLOW	☐	5. YELLOW ORANGE	☐	6. LIGHT ORANGE
☐	7. MEDIUM ORANGE	☐	8. DARK ORANGE	☐	9. ORANGE RED
☐	10. PINK	☐	11. MEDIUM RED	☐	12. DARK RED
☐	13. LIGHT GREEN	☐	14. MEDIUM GREEN	☐	15. DARK GREEN
☐	16. GREEN BLUE	☐	17. LIGHT BLUE	☐	18. MEDIUM BLUE
☐	19. DARK BLUE	☐	20. BLUE PURPLE	☐	21. LIGHT PURPLE
☐	22. MEDIUM PURPLE	☐	23. DARK PURPLE	☐	24. LIGHT BROWN
☐	25. MEDIUM BROWN	☐	26. DARK BROWN	☐	27. LIGHT GRAY
☐	28. MEDIUM GRAY	☐	29. DARK GRAY	☐	30. BLACK

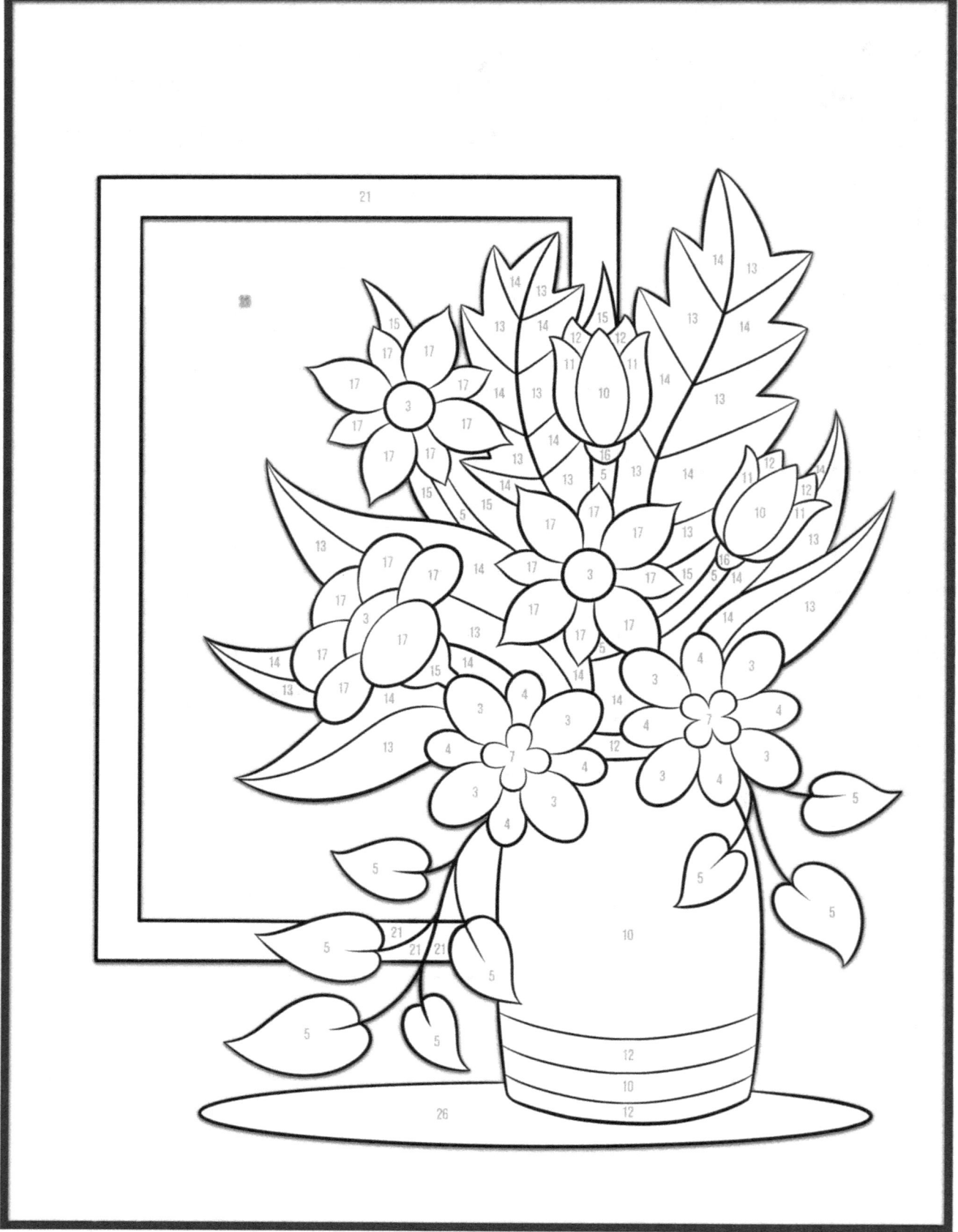

CUSTOM COLOR CHART

☐	1. WHITE	☐	2. LIGHT YELLOW	☐	3. MEDIUM YELLOW
☐	4. DARK YELLOW	☐	5. YELLOW ORANGE	☐	6. LIGHT ORANGE
☐	7. MEDIUM ORANGE	☐	8. DARK ORANGE	☐	9. ORANGE RED
☐	10. PINK	☐	11. MEDIUM RED	☐	12. DARK RED
☐	13. LIGHT GREEN	☐	14. MEDIUM GREEN	☐	15. DARK GREEN
☐	16. GREEN BLUE	☐	17. LIGHT BLUE	☐	18. MEDIUM BLUE
☐	19. DARK BLUE	☐	20. BLUE PURPLE	☐	21. LIGHT PURPLE
☐	22. MEDIUM PURPLE	☐	23. DARK PURPLE	☐	24. LIGHT BROWN
☐	25. MEDIUM BROWN	☐	26. DARK BROWN	☐	27. LIGHT GRAY
☐	28. MEDIUM GRAY	☐	29. DARK GRAY	☐	30. BLACK

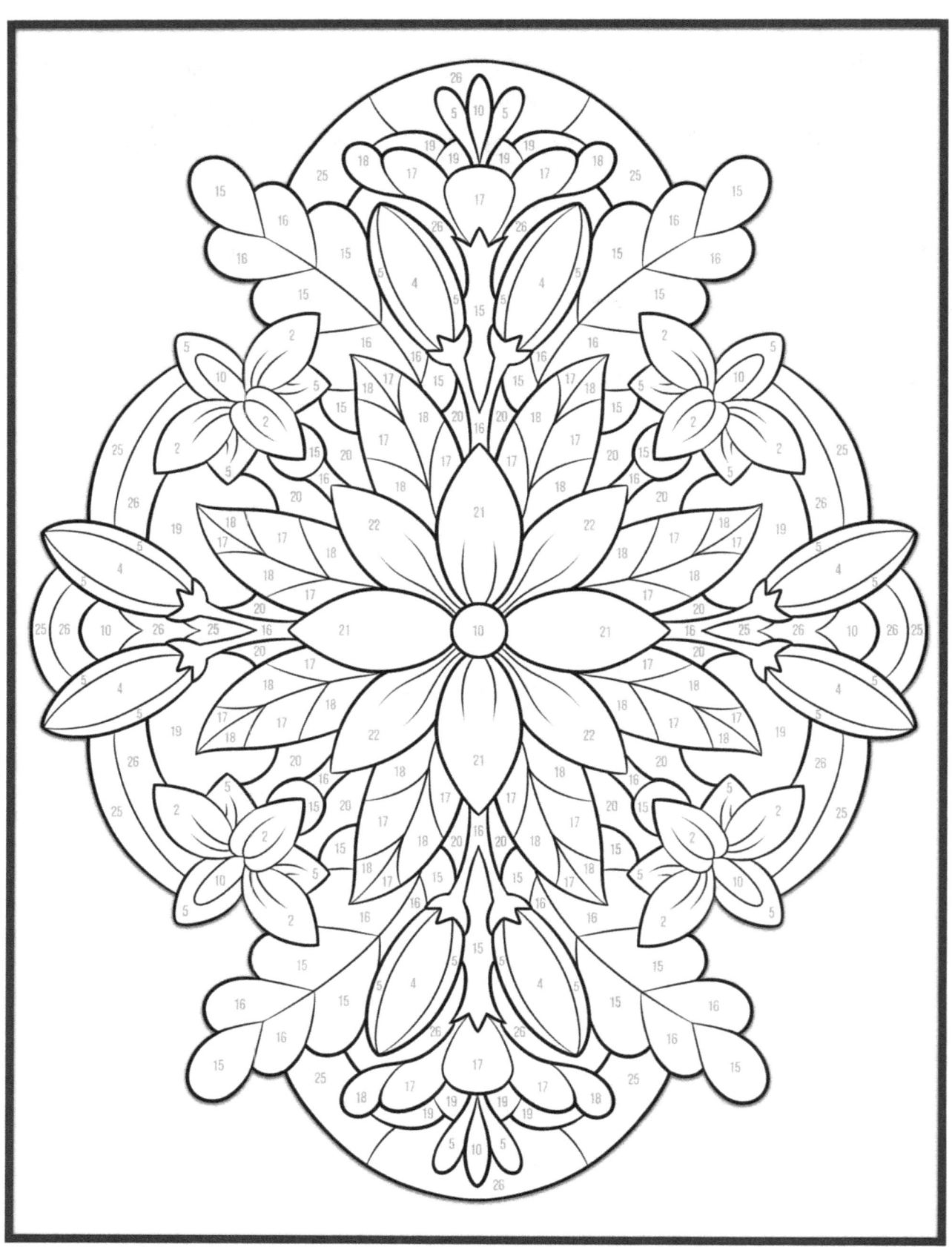

CUSTOM COLOR CHART

☐	1. WHITE	☐	2. LIGHT YELLOW	☐	3. MEDIUM YELLOW
☐	4. DARK YELLOW	☐	5. YELLOW ORANGE	☐	6. LIGHT ORANGE
☐	7. MEDIUM ORANGE	☐	8. DARK ORANGE	☐	9. ORANGE RED
☐	10. PINK	☐	11. MEDIUM RED	☐	12. DARK RED
☐	13. LIGHT GREEN	☐	14. MEDIUM GREEN	☐	15. DARK GREEN
☐	16. GREEN BLUE	☐	17. LIGHT BLUE	☐	18. MEDIUM BLUE
☐	19. DARK BLUE	☐	20. BLUE PURPLE	☐	21. LIGHT PURPLE
☐	22. MEDIUM PURPLE	☐	23. DARK PURPLE	☐	24. LIGHT BROWN
☐	25. MEDIUM BROWN	☐	26. DARK BROWN	☐	27. LIGHT GRAY
☐	28. MEDIUM GRAY	☐	29. DARK GRAY	☐	30. BLACK

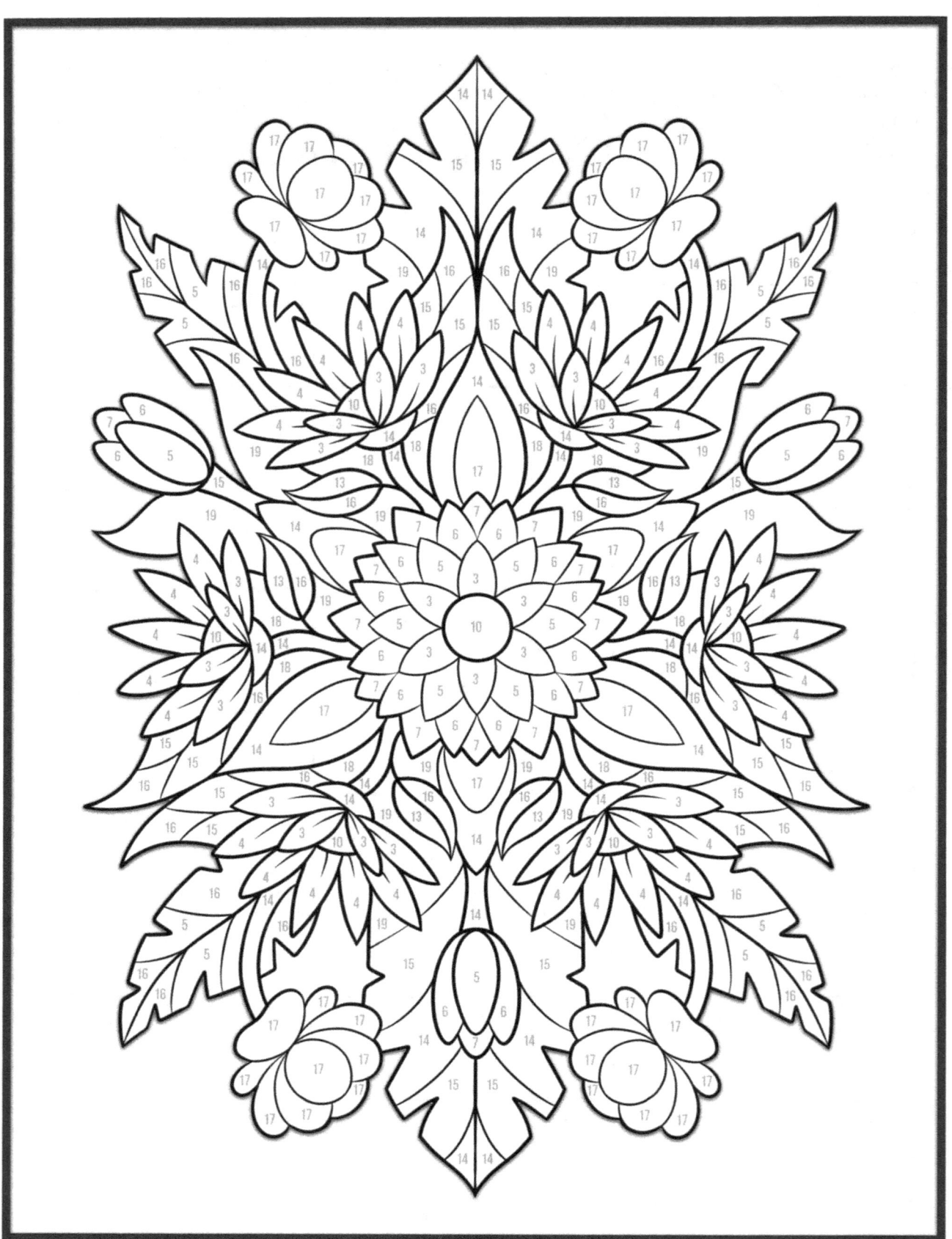

CUSTOM COLOR CHART

☐ 1. WHITE	☐ 2. LIGHT YELLOW	☐ 3. MEDIUM YELLOW
☐ 4. DARK YELLOW	☐ 5. YELLOW ORANGE	☐ 6. LIGHT ORANGE
☐ 7. MEDIUM ORANGE	☐ 8. DARK ORANGE	☐ 9. ORANGE RED
☐ 10. PINK	☐ 11. MEDIUM RED	☐ 12. DARK RED
☐ 13. LIGHT GREEN	☐ 14. MEDIUM GREEN	☐ 15. DARK GREEN
☐ 16. GREEN BLUE	☐ 17. LIGHT BLUE	☐ 18. MEDIUM BLUE
☐ 19. DARK BLUE	☐ 20. BLUE PURPLE	☐ 21. LIGHT PURPLE
☐ 22. MEDIUM PURPLE	☐ 23. DARK PURPLE	☐ 24. LIGHT BROWN
☐ 25. MEDIUM BROWN	☐ 26. DARK BROWN	☐ 27. LIGHT GRAY
☐ 28. MEDIUM GRAY	☐ 29. DARK GRAY	☐ 30. BLACK

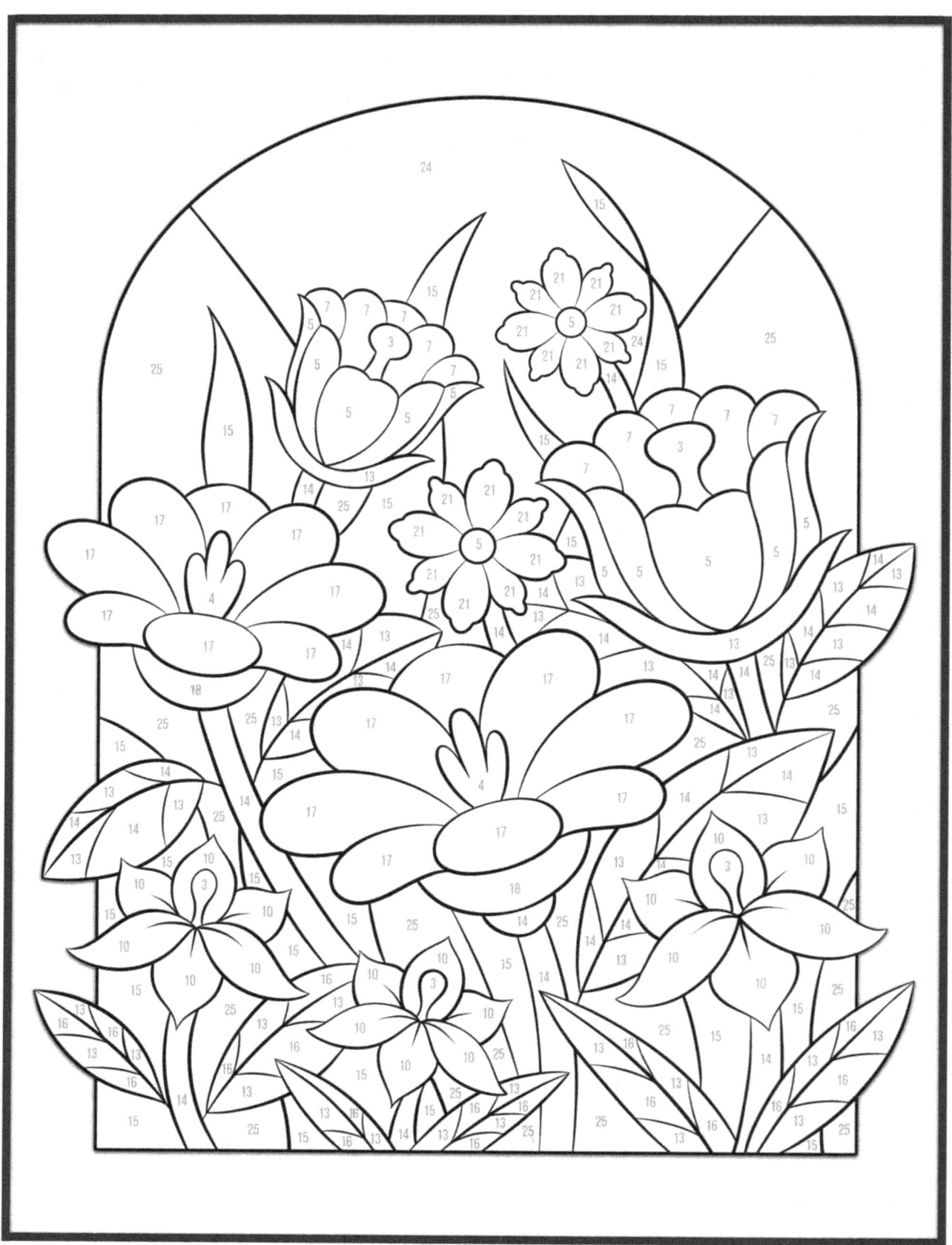

CUSTOM COLOR CHART

1. WHITE
_____

2. LIGHT YELLOW
_____

3. MEDIUM YELLOW
_____

4. DARK YELLOW
_____

5. YELLOW ORANGE
_____

6. LIGHT ORANGE
_____

7. MEDIUM ORANGE
_____

8. DARK ORANGE
_____

9. ORANGE RED
_____

10. PINK
_____

11. MEDIUM RED
_____

12. DARK RED
_____

13. LIGHT GREEN
_____

14. MEDIUM GREEN
_____

15. DARK GREEN
_____

16. GREEN BLUE
_____

17. LIGHT BLUE
_____

18. MEDIUM BLUE
_____

19. DARK BLUE
_____

20. BLUE PURPLE
_____

21. LIGHT PURPLE
_____

22. MEDIUM PURPLE
_____

23. DARK PURPLE
_____

24. LIGHT BROWN
_____

25. MEDIUM BROWN
_____

26. DARK BROWN
_____

27. LIGHT GRAY
_____

28. MEDIUM GRAY
_____

29. DARK GRAY
_____

30. BLACK
_____

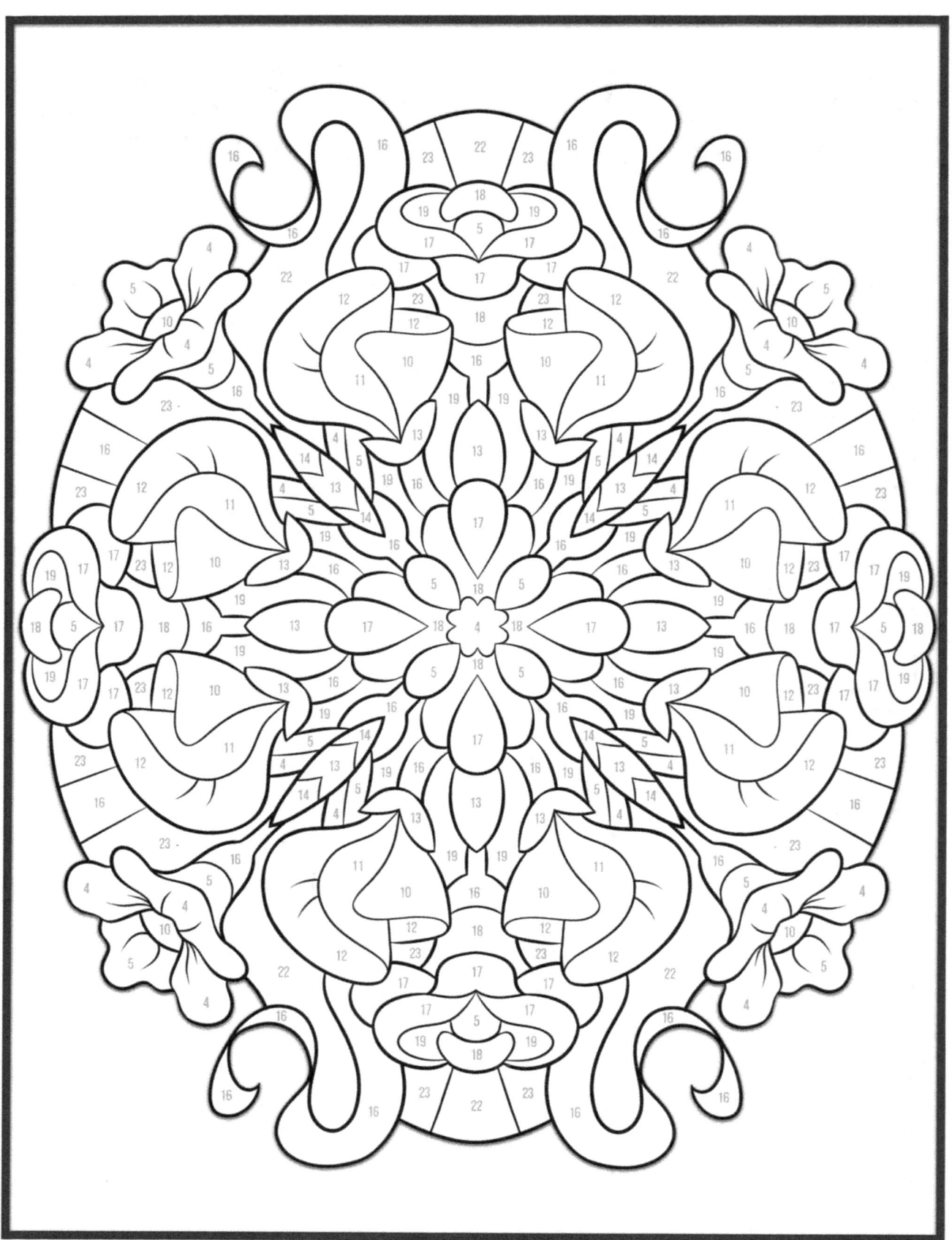

CUSTOM COLOR CHART

1. WHITE

2. LIGHT YELLOW

3. MEDIUM YELLOW

4. DARK YELLOW

5. YELLOW ORANGE

6. LIGHT ORANGE

7. MEDIUM ORANGE

8. DARK ORANGE

9. ORANGE RED

10. PINK

11. MEDIUM RED

12. DARK RED

13. LIGHT GREEN

14. MEDIUM GREEN

15. DARK GREEN

16. GREEN BLUE

17. LIGHT BLUE

18. MEDIUM BLUE

19. DARK BLUE

20. BLUE PURPLE

21. LIGHT PURPLE

22. MEDIUM PURPLE

23. DARK PURPLE

24. LIGHT BROWN

25. MEDIUM BROWN

26. DARK BROWN

27. LIGHT GRAY

28. MEDIUM GRAY

29. DARK GRAY

30. BLACK

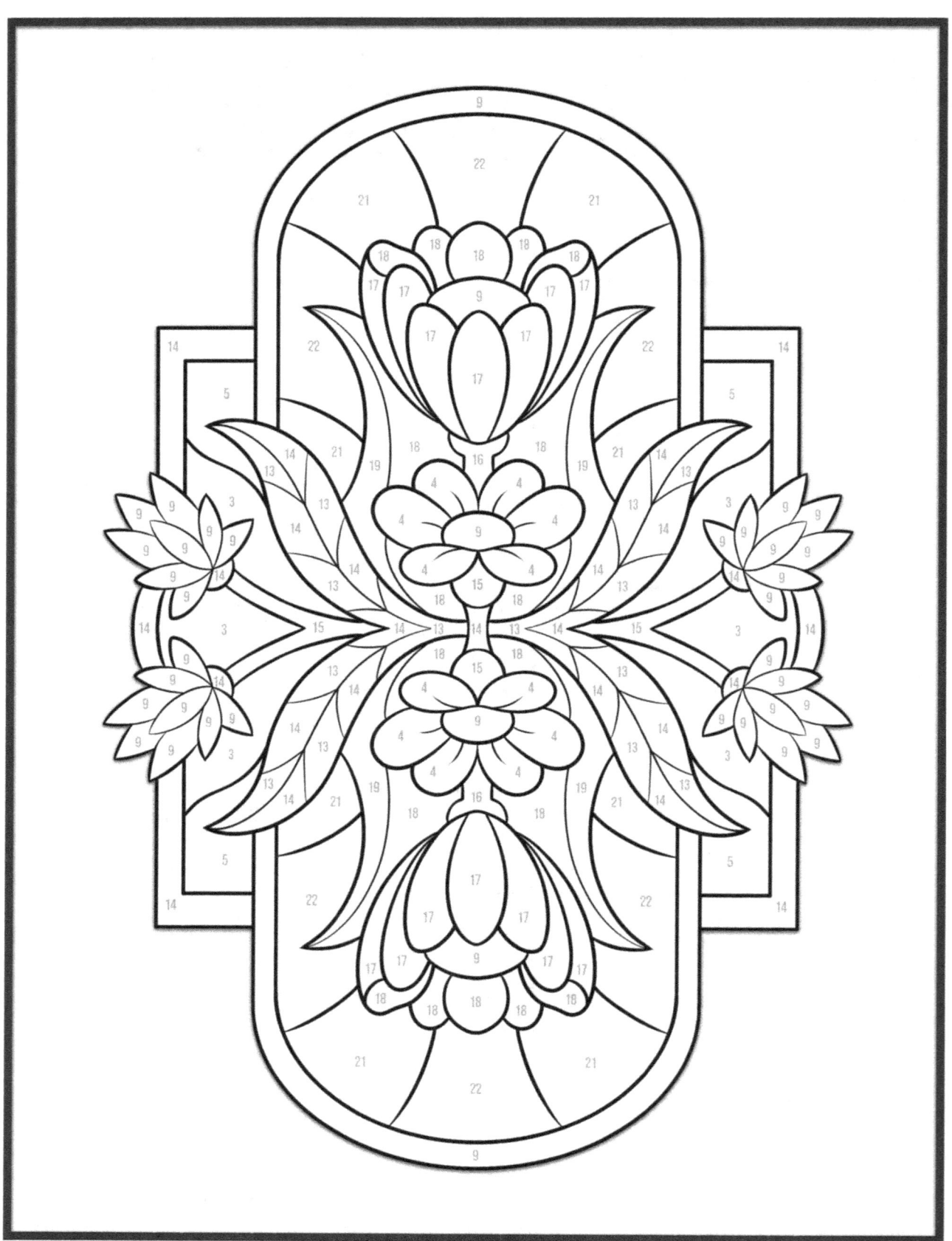

CUSTOM COLOR CHART

1. WHITE

2. LIGHT YELLOW

3. MEDIUM YELLOW

4. DARK YELLOW

5. YELLOW ORANGE

6. LIGHT ORANGE

7. MEDIUM ORANGE

8. DARK ORANGE

9. ORANGE RED

10. PINK

11. MEDIUM RED

12. DARK RED

13. LIGHT GREEN

14. MEDIUM GREEN

15. DARK GREEN

16. GREEN BLUE

17. LIGHT BLUE

18. MEDIUM BLUE

19. DARK BLUE

20. BLUE PURPLE

21. LIGHT PURPLE

22. MEDIUM PURPLE

23. DARK PURPLE

24. LIGHT BROWN

25. MEDIUM BROWN

26. DARK BROWN

27. LIGHT GRAY

28. MEDIUM GRAY

29. DARK GRAY

30. BLACK

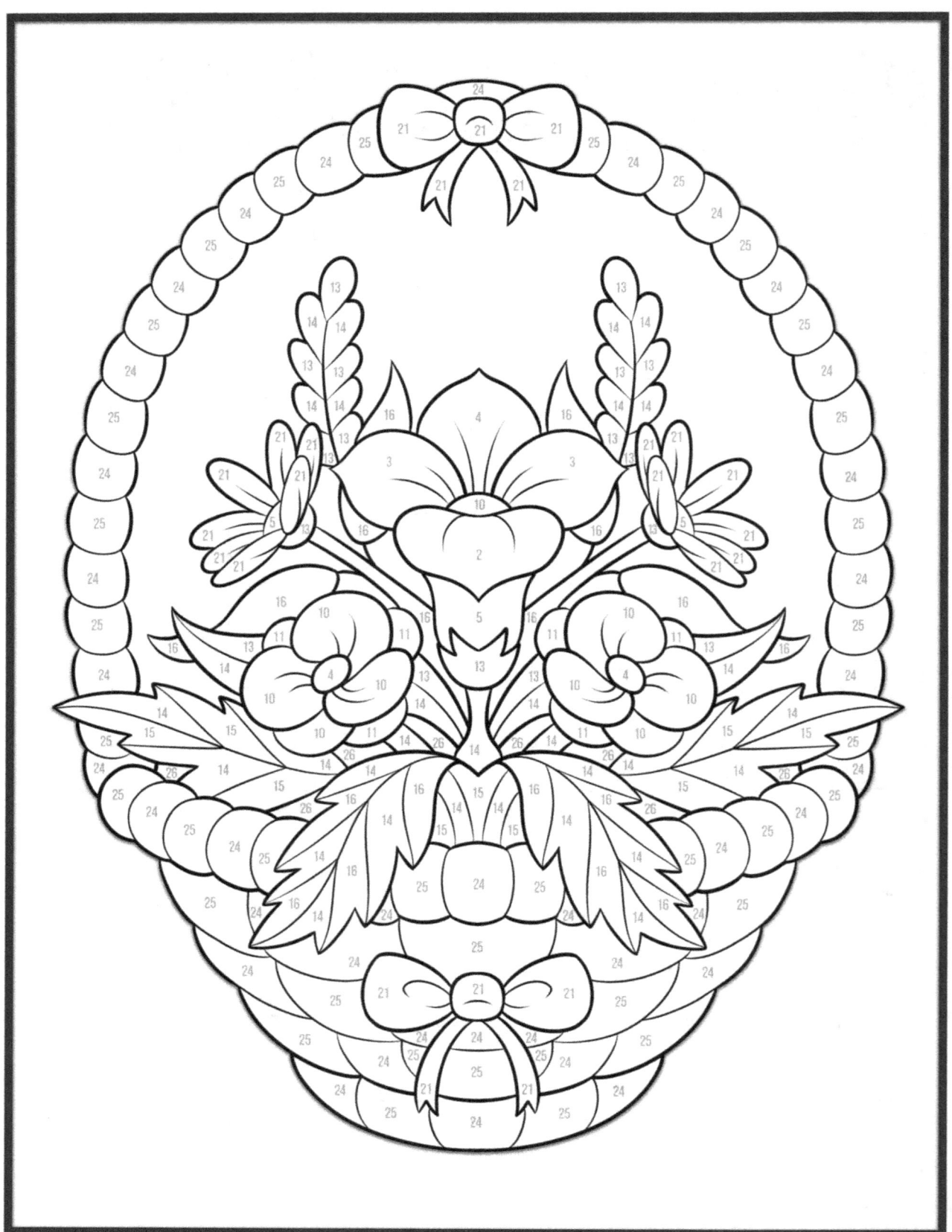

CUSTOM COLOR CHART

1. WHITE
_____

2. LIGHT YELLOW
_____

3. MEDIUM YELLOW
_____

4. DARK YELLOW
_____

5. YELLOW ORANGE
_____

6. LIGHT ORANGE
_____

7. MEDIUM ORANGE
_____

8. DARK ORANGE
_____

9. ORANGE RED
_____

10. PINK
_____

11. MEDIUM RED
_____

12. DARK RED
_____

13. LIGHT GREEN
_____

14. MEDIUM GREEN
_____

15. DARK GREEN
_____

16. GREEN BLUE
_____

17. LIGHT BLUE
_____

18. MEDIUM BLUE
_____

19. DARK BLUE
_____

20. BLUE PURPLE
_____

21. LIGHT PURPLE
_____

22. MEDIUM PURPLE
_____

23. DARK PURPLE
_____

24. LIGHT BROWN
_____

25. MEDIUM BROWN
_____

26. DARK BROWN
_____

27. LIGHT GRAY
_____

28. MEDIUM GRAY
_____

29. DARK GRAY
_____

30. BLACK
_____

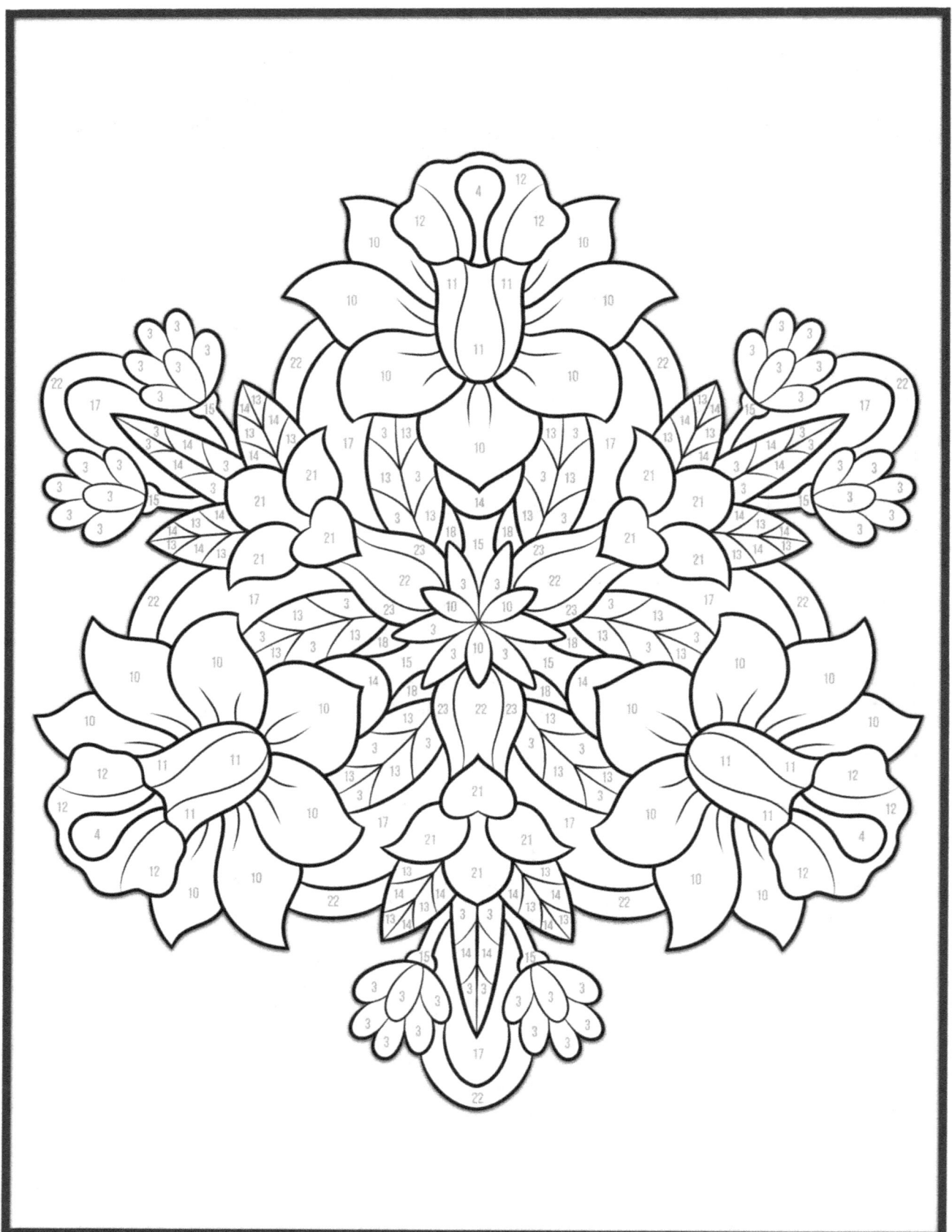

CUSTOM COLOR CHART

1. WHITE

2. LIGHT YELLOW

3. MEDIUM YELLOW

4. DARK YELLOW

5. YELLOW ORANGE

6. LIGHT ORANGE

7. MEDIUM ORANGE

8. DARK ORANGE

9. ORANGE RED

10. PINK

11. MEDIUM RED

12. DARK RED

13. LIGHT GREEN

14. MEDIUM GREEN

15. DARK GREEN

16. GREEN BLUE

17. LIGHT BLUE

18. MEDIUM BLUE

19. DARK BLUE

20. BLUE PURPLE

21. LIGHT PURPLE

22. MEDIUM PURPLE

23. DARK PURPLE

24. LIGHT BROWN

25. MEDIUM BROWN

26. DARK BROWN

27. LIGHT GRAY

28. MEDIUM GRAY

29. DARK GRAY

30. BLACK

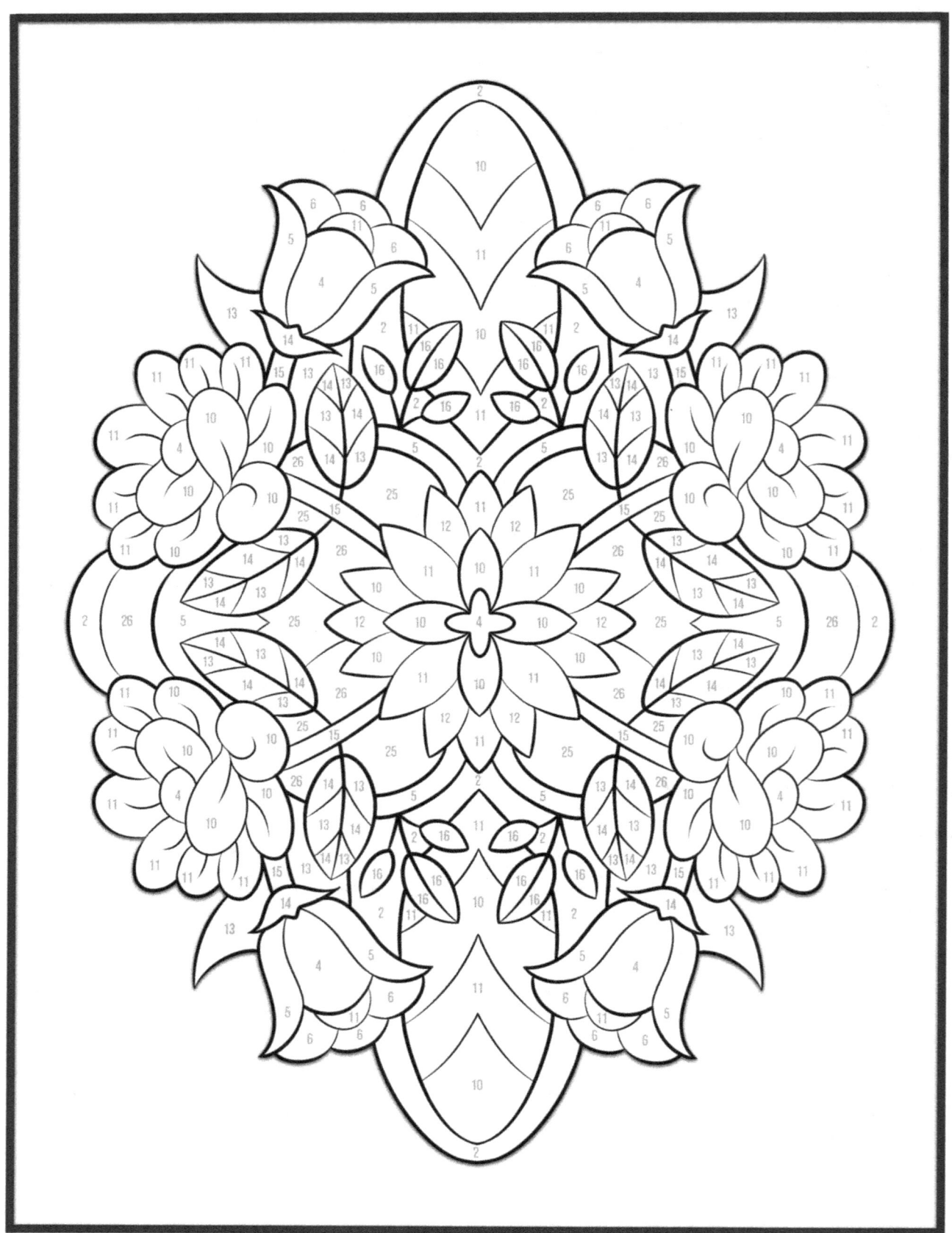

CUSTOM COLOR CHART

☐	1. WHITE	☐	2. LIGHT YELLOW	☐	3. MEDIUM YELLOW
☐	4. DARK YELLOW	☐	5. YELLOW ORANGE	☐	6. LIGHT ORANGE
☐	7. MEDIUM ORANGE	☐	8. DARK ORANGE	☐	9. ORANGE RED
☐	10. PINK	☐	11. MEDIUM RED	☐	12. DARK RED
☐	13. LIGHT GREEN	☐	14. MEDIUM GREEN	☐	15. DARK GREEN
☐	16. GREEN BLUE	☐	17. LIGHT BLUE	☐	18. MEDIUM BLUE
☐	19. DARK BLUE	☐	20. BLUE PURPLE	☐	21. LIGHT PURPLE
☐	22. MEDIUM PURPLE	☐	23. DARK PURPLE	☐	24. LIGHT BROWN
☐	25. MEDIUM BROWN	☐	26. DARK BROWN	☐	27. LIGHT GRAY
☐	28. MEDIUM GRAY	☐	29. DARK GRAY	☐	30. BLACK

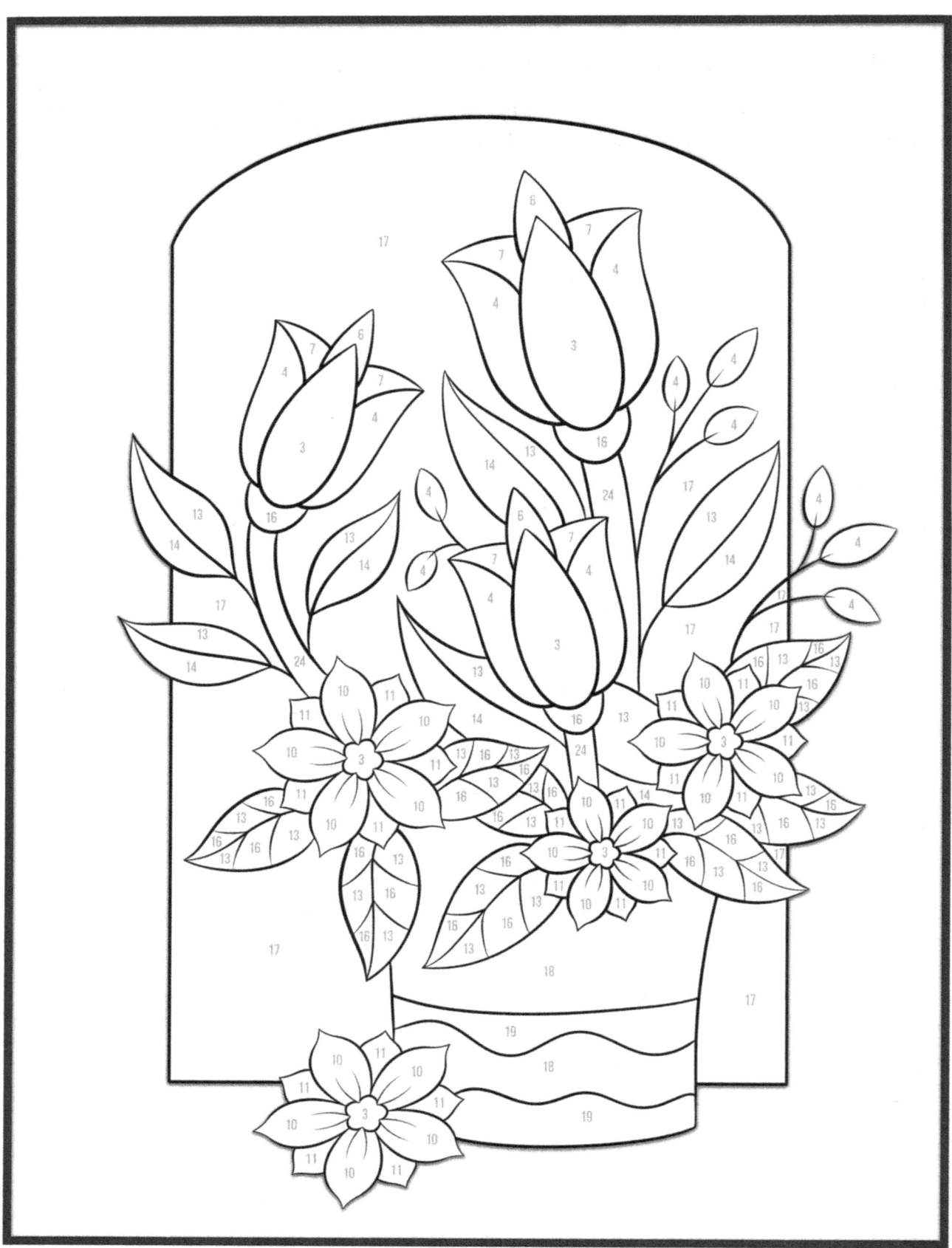

CUSTOM COLOR CHART

☐ 1. WHITE

☐ 2. LIGHT YELLOW

☐ 3. MEDIUM YELLOW

☐ 4. DARK YELLOW

☐ 5. YELLOW ORANGE

☐ 6. LIGHT ORANGE

☐ 7. MEDIUM ORANGE

☐ 8. DARK ORANGE

☐ 9. ORANGE RED

☐ 10. PINK

☐ 11. MEDIUM RED

☐ 12. DARK RED

☐ 13. LIGHT GREEN

☐ 14. MEDIUM GREEN

☐ 15. DARK GREEN

☐ 16. GREEN BLUE

☐ 17. LIGHT BLUE

☐ 18. MEDIUM BLUE

☐ 19. DARK BLUE

☐ 20. BLUE PURPLE

☐ 21. LIGHT PURPLE

☐ 22. MEDIUM PURPLE

☐ 23. DARK PURPLE

☐ 24. LIGHT BROWN

☐ 25. MEDIUM BROWN

☐ 26. DARK BROWN

☐ 27. LIGHT GRAY

☐ 28. MEDIUM GRAY

☐ 29. DARK GRAY

☐ 30. BLACK

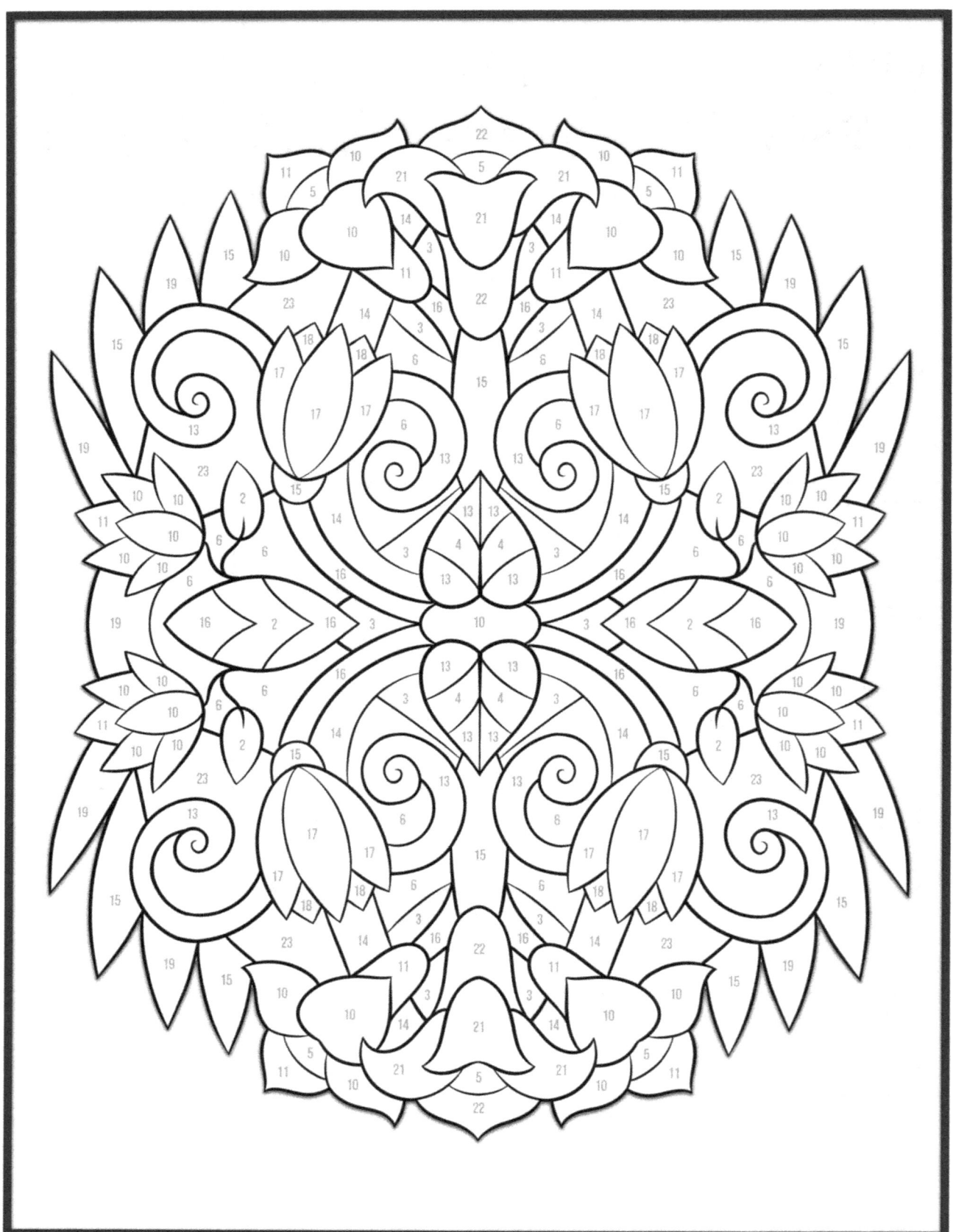

CUSTOM COLOR CHART

1. WHITE

2. LIGHT YELLOW

3. MEDIUM YELLOW

4. DARK YELLOW

5. YELLOW ORANGE

6. LIGHT ORANGE

7. MEDIUM ORANGE

8. DARK ORANGE

9. ORANGE RED

10. PINK

11. MEDIUM RED

12. DARK RED

13. LIGHT GREEN

14. MEDIUM GREEN

15. DARK GREEN

16. GREEN BLUE

17. LIGHT BLUE

18. MEDIUM BLUE

19. DARK BLUE

20. BLUE PURPLE

21. LIGHT PURPLE

22. MEDIUM PURPLE

23. DARK PURPLE

24. LIGHT BROWN

25. MEDIUM BROWN

26. DARK BROWN

27. LIGHT GRAY

28. MEDIUM GRAY

29. DARK GRAY

30. BLACK

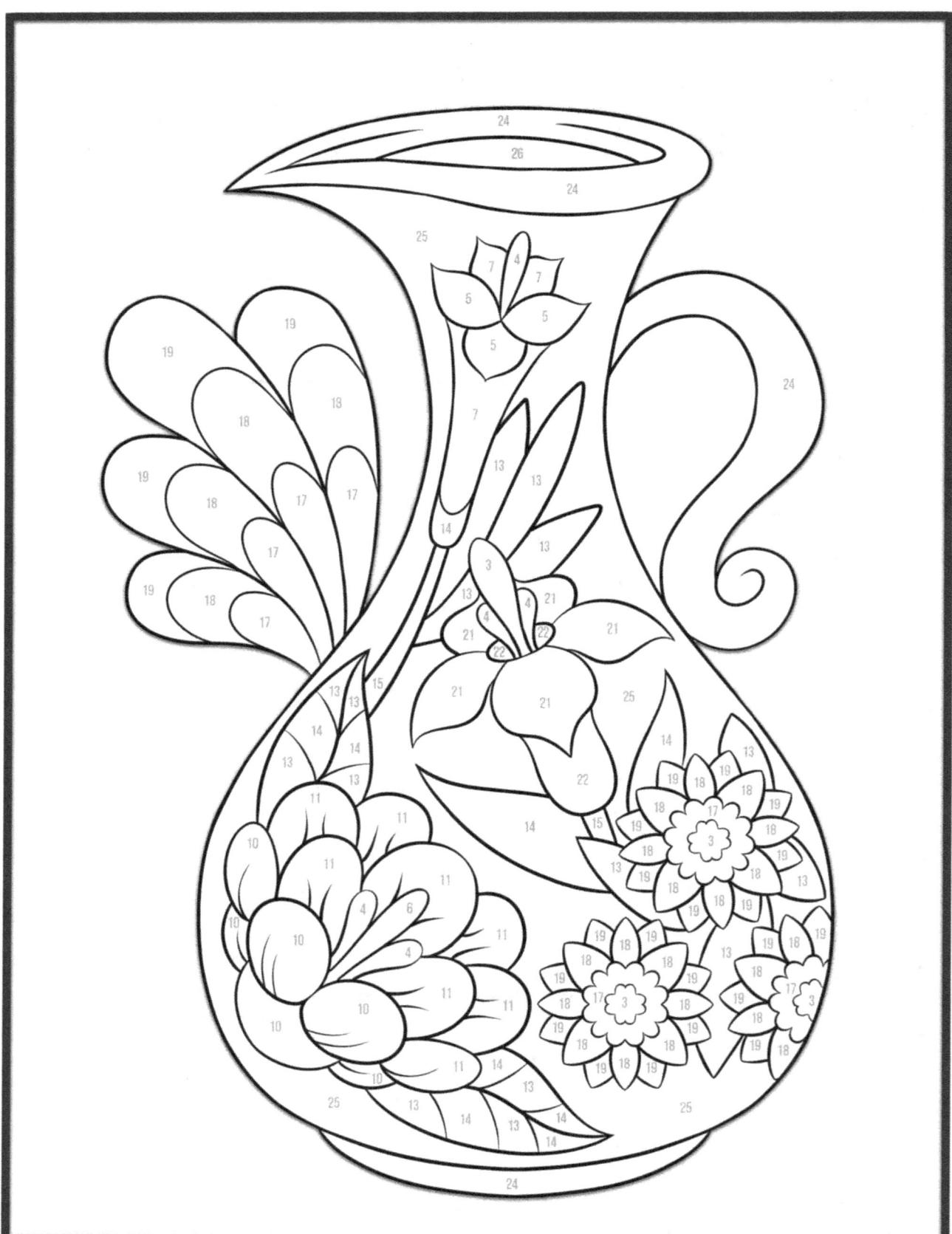

CUSTOM COLOR CHART

1. WHITE	2. LIGHT YELLOW	3. MEDIUM YELLOW
4. DARK YELLOW	5. YELLOW ORANGE	6. LIGHT ORANGE
7. MEDIUM ORANGE	8. DARK ORANGE	9. ORANGE RED
10. PINK	11. MEDIUM RED	12. DARK RED
13. LIGHT GREEN	14. MEDIUM GREEN	15. DARK GREEN
16. GREEN BLUE	17. LIGHT BLUE	18. MEDIUM BLUE
19. DARK BLUE	20. BLUE PURPLE	21. LIGHT PURPLE
22. MEDIUM PURPLE	23. DARK PURPLE	24. LIGHT BROWN
25. MEDIUM BROWN	26. DARK BROWN	27. LIGHT GRAY
28. MEDIUM GRAY	29. DARK GRAY	30. BLACK

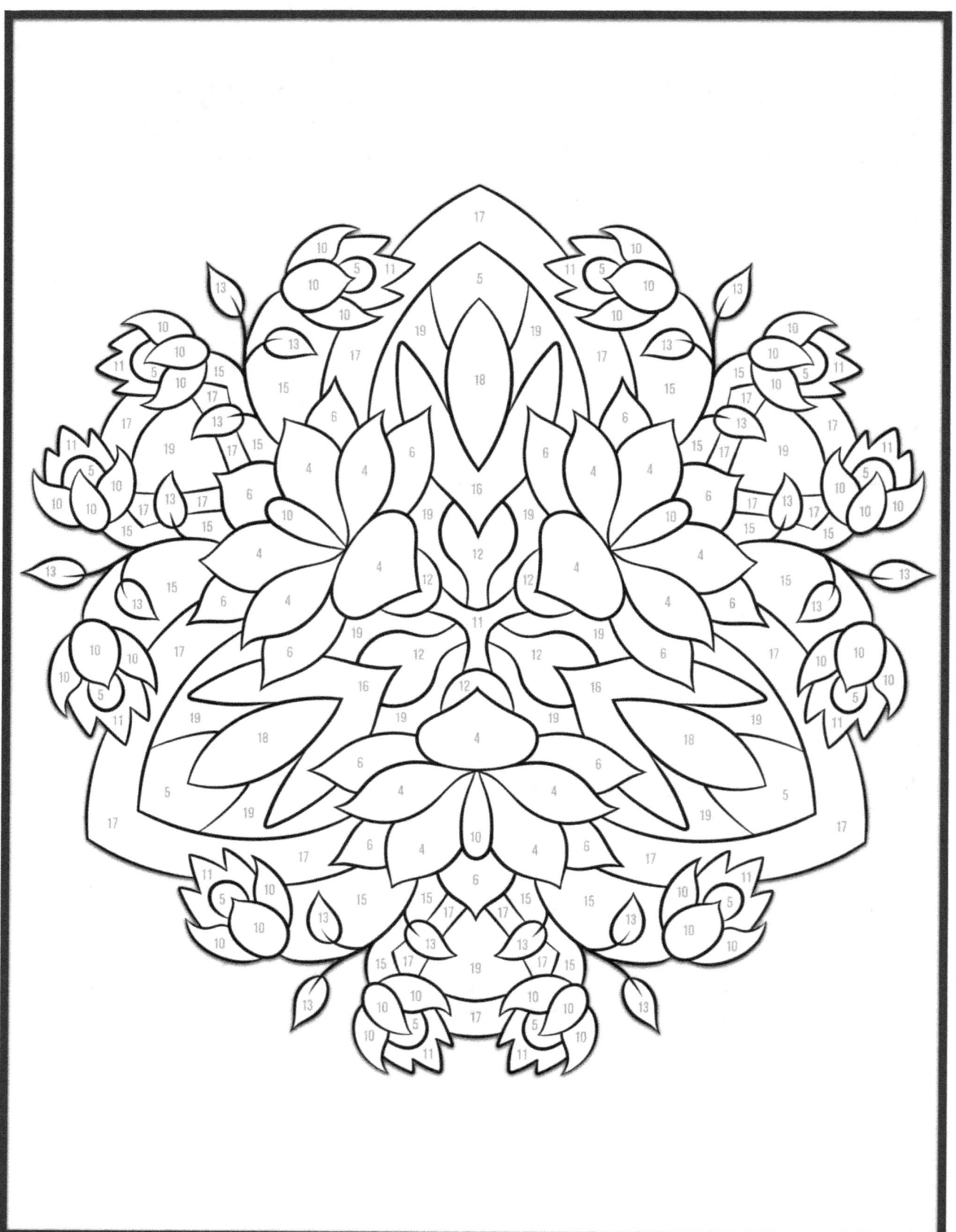

CUSTOM COLOR CHART

☐	1. WHITE	☐	2. LIGHT YELLOW	☐	3. MEDIUM YELLOW
☐	4. DARK YELLOW	☐	5. YELLOW ORANGE	☐	6. LIGHT ORANGE
☐	7. MEDIUM ORANGE	☐	8. DARK ORANGE	☐	9. ORANGE RED
☐	10. PINK	☐	11. MEDIUM RED	☐	12. DARK RED
☐	13. LIGHT GREEN	☐	14. MEDIUM GREEN	☐	15. DARK GREEN
☐	16. GREEN BLUE	☐	17. LIGHT BLUE	☐	18. MEDIUM BLUE
☐	19. DARK BLUE	☐	20. BLUE PURPLE	☐	21. LIGHT PURPLE
☐	22. MEDIUM PURPLE	☐	23. DARK PURPLE	☐	24. LIGHT BROWN
☐	25. MEDIUM BROWN	☐	26. DARK BROWN	☐	27. LIGHT GRAY
☐	28. MEDIUM GRAY	☐	29. DARK GRAY	☐	30. BLACK

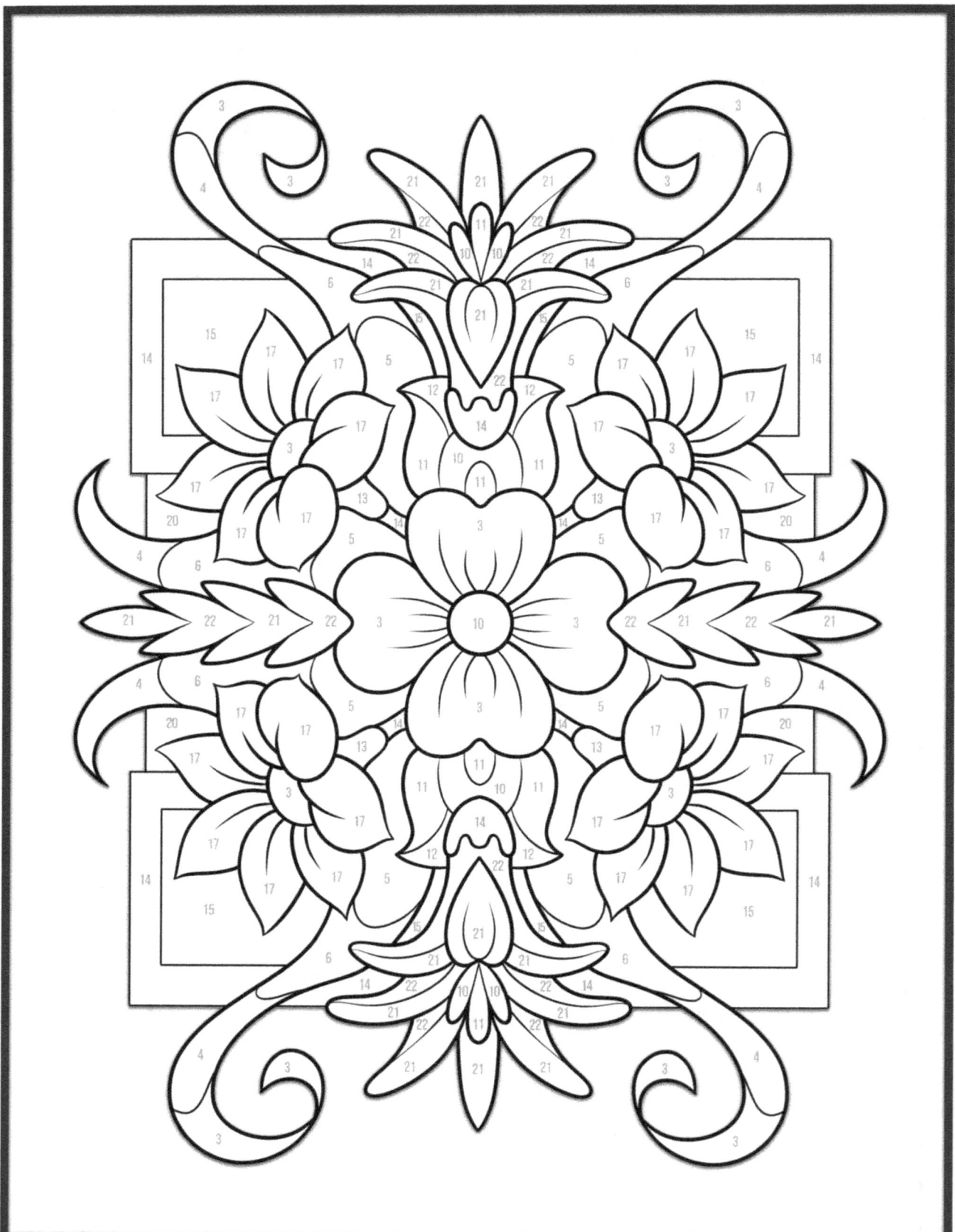

CUSTOM COLOR CHART

1. WHITE

2. LIGHT YELLOW

3. MEDIUM YELLOW

4. DARK YELLOW

5. YELLOW ORANGE

6. LIGHT ORANGE

7. MEDIUM ORANGE

8. DARK ORANGE

9. ORANGE RED

10. PINK

11. MEDIUM RED

12. DARK RED

13. LIGHT GREEN

14. MEDIUM GREEN

15. DARK GREEN

16. GREEN BLUE

17. LIGHT BLUE

18. MEDIUM BLUE

19. DARK BLUE

20. BLUE PURPLE

21. LIGHT PURPLE

22. MEDIUM PURPLE

23. DARK PURPLE

24. LIGHT BROWN

25. MEDIUM BROWN

26. DARK BROWN

27. LIGHT GRAY

28. MEDIUM GRAY

29. DARK GRAY

30. BLACK

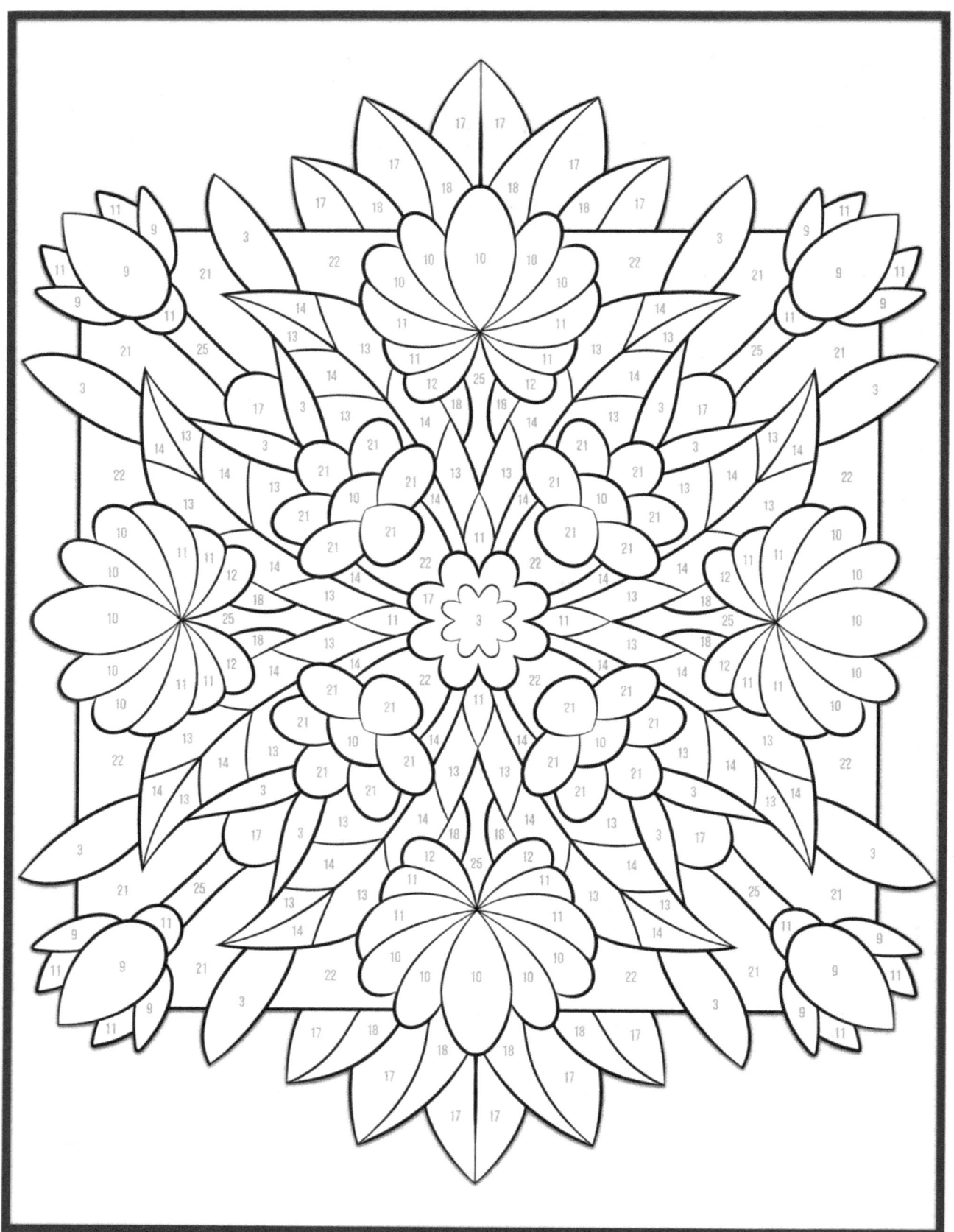

CUSTOM COLOR CHART

1. WHITE	2. LIGHT YELLOW	3. MEDIUM YELLOW
4. DARK YELLOW	5. YELLOW ORANGE	6. LIGHT ORANGE
7. MEDIUM ORANGE	8. DARK ORANGE	9. ORANGE RED
10. PINK	11. MEDIUM RED	12. DARK RED
13. LIGHT GREEN	14. MEDIUM GREEN	15. DARK GREEN
16. GREEN BLUE	17. LIGHT BLUE	18. MEDIUM BLUE
19. DARK BLUE	20. BLUE PURPLE	21. LIGHT PURPLE
22. MEDIUM PURPLE	23. DARK PURPLE	24. LIGHT BROWN
25. MEDIUM BROWN	26. DARK BROWN	27. LIGHT GRAY
28. MEDIUM GRAY	29. DARK GRAY	30. BLACK

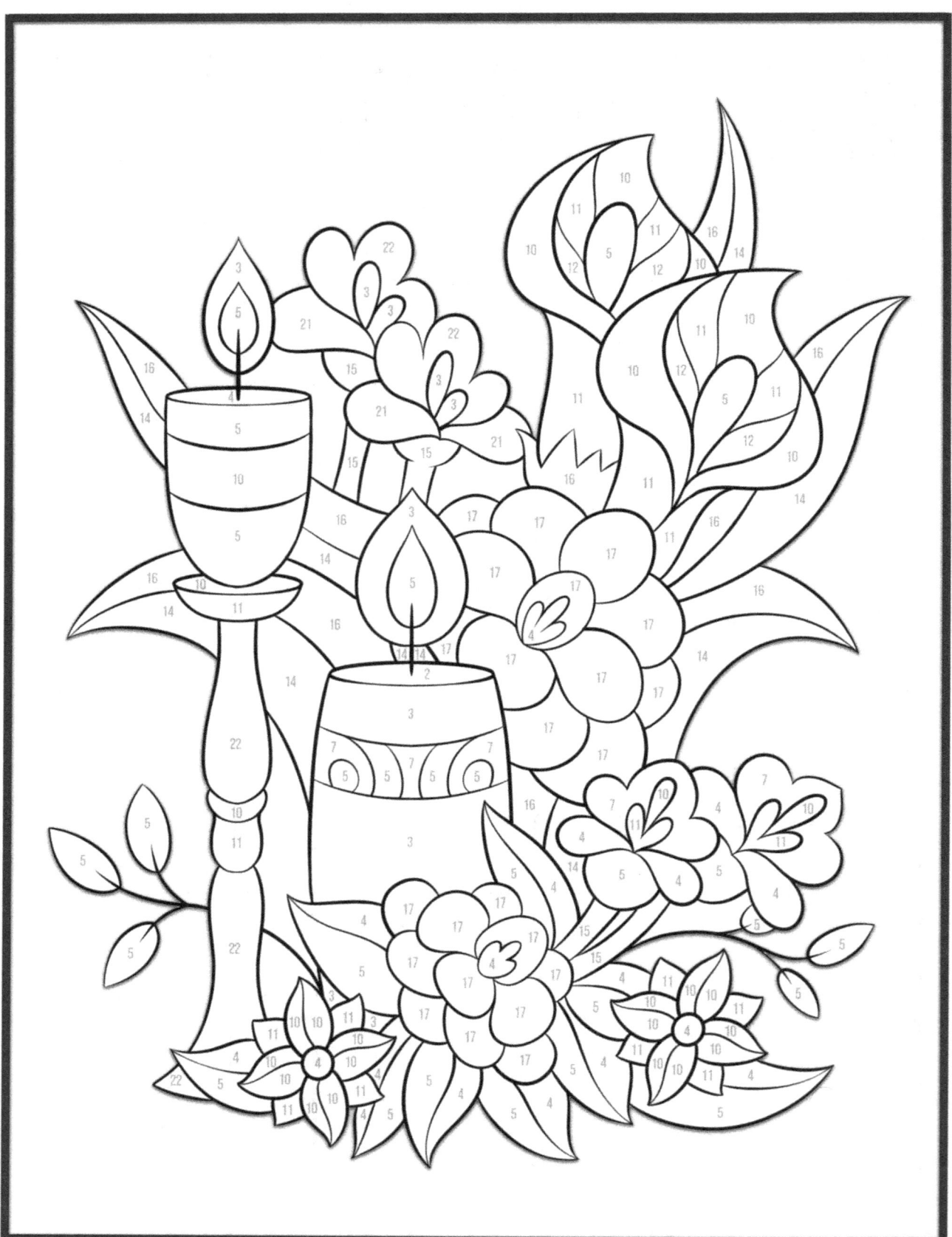

CUSTOM COLOR CHART

☐	1. WHITE	☐	2. LIGHT YELLOW	☐	3. MEDIUM YELLOW
☐	4. DARK YELLOW	☐	5. YELLOW ORANGE	☐	6. LIGHT ORANGE
☐	7. MEDIUM ORANGE	☐	8. DARK ORANGE	☐	9. ORANGE RED
☐	10. PINK	☐	11. MEDIUM RED	☐	12. DARK RED
☐	13. LIGHT GREEN	☐	14. MEDIUM GREEN	☐	15. DARK GREEN
☐	16. GREEN BLUE	☐	17. LIGHT BLUE	☐	18. MEDIUM BLUE
☐	19. DARK BLUE	☐	20. BLUE PURPLE	☐	21. LIGHT PURPLE
☐	22. MEDIUM PURPLE	☐	23. DARK PURPLE	☐	24. LIGHT BROWN
☐	25. MEDIUM BROWN	☐	26. DARK BROWN	☐	27. LIGHT GRAY
☐	28. MEDIUM GRAY	☐	29. DARK GRAY	☐	30. BLACK

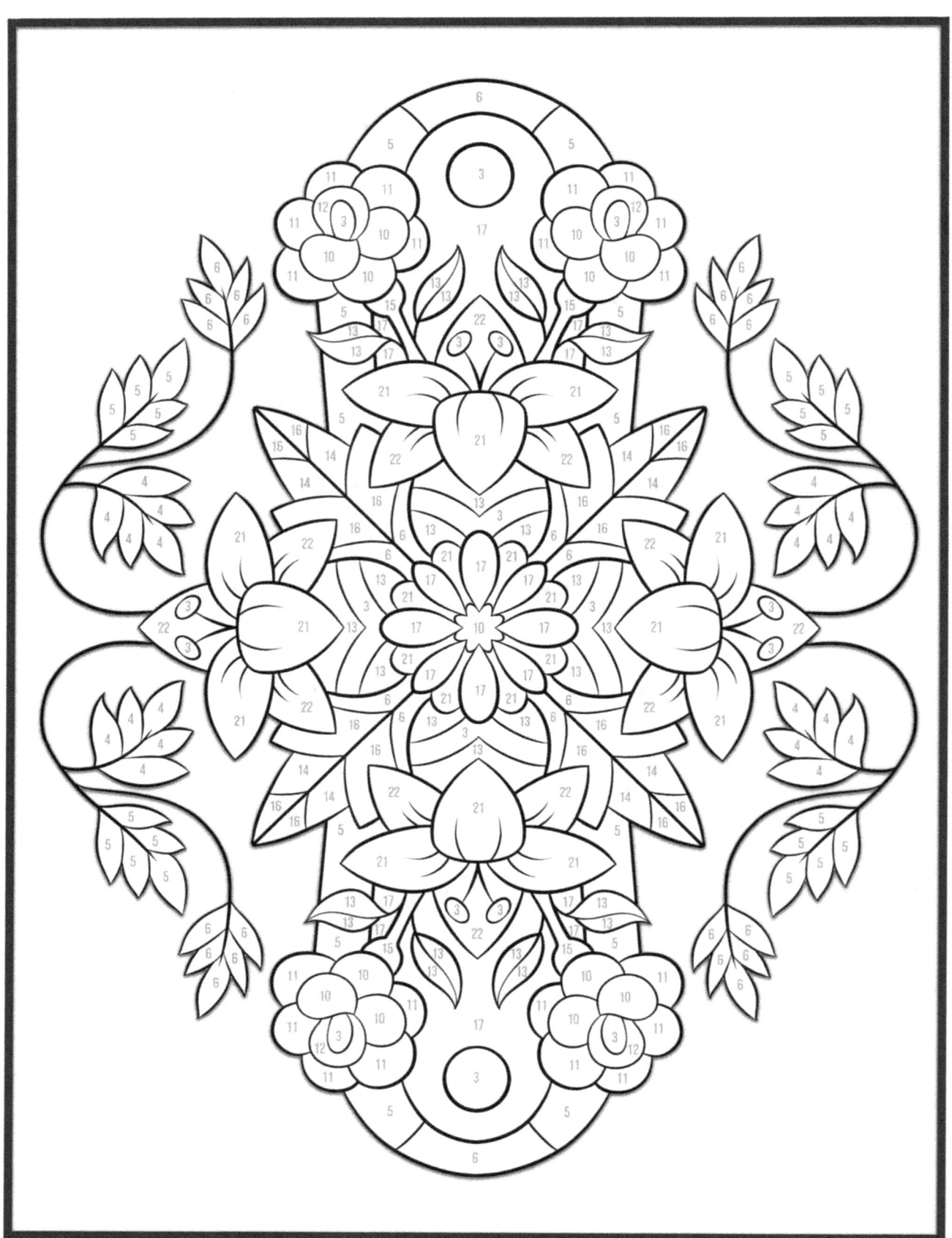

CUSTOM COLOR CHART

☐ 1. WHITE
_____

☐ 2. LIGHT YELLOW
_____

☐ 3. MEDIUM YELLOW
_____

☐ 4. DARK YELLOW
_____

☐ 5. YELLOW ORANGE
_____

☐ 6. LIGHT ORANGE
_____

☐ 7. MEDIUM ORANGE
_____

☐ 8. DARK ORANGE
_____

☐ 9. ORANGE RED
_____

☐ 10. PINK
_____

☐ 11. MEDIUM RED
_____

☐ 12. DARK RED
_____

☐ 13. LIGHT GREEN
_____

☐ 14. MEDIUM GREEN
_____

☐ 15. DARK GREEN
_____

☐ 16. GREEN BLUE
_____

☐ 17. LIGHT BLUE
_____

☐ 18. MEDIUM BLUE
_____

☐ 19. DARK BLUE
_____

☐ 20. BLUE PURPLE
_____

☐ 21. LIGHT PURPLE
_____

☐ 22. MEDIUM PURPLE
_____

☐ 23. DARK PURPLE
_____

☐ 24. LIGHT BROWN
_____

☐ 25. MEDIUM BROWN
_____

☐ 26. DARK BROWN
_____

☐ 27. LIGHT GRAY
_____

☐ 28. MEDIUM GRAY
_____

☐ 29. DARK GRAY
_____

☐ 30. BLACK
_____

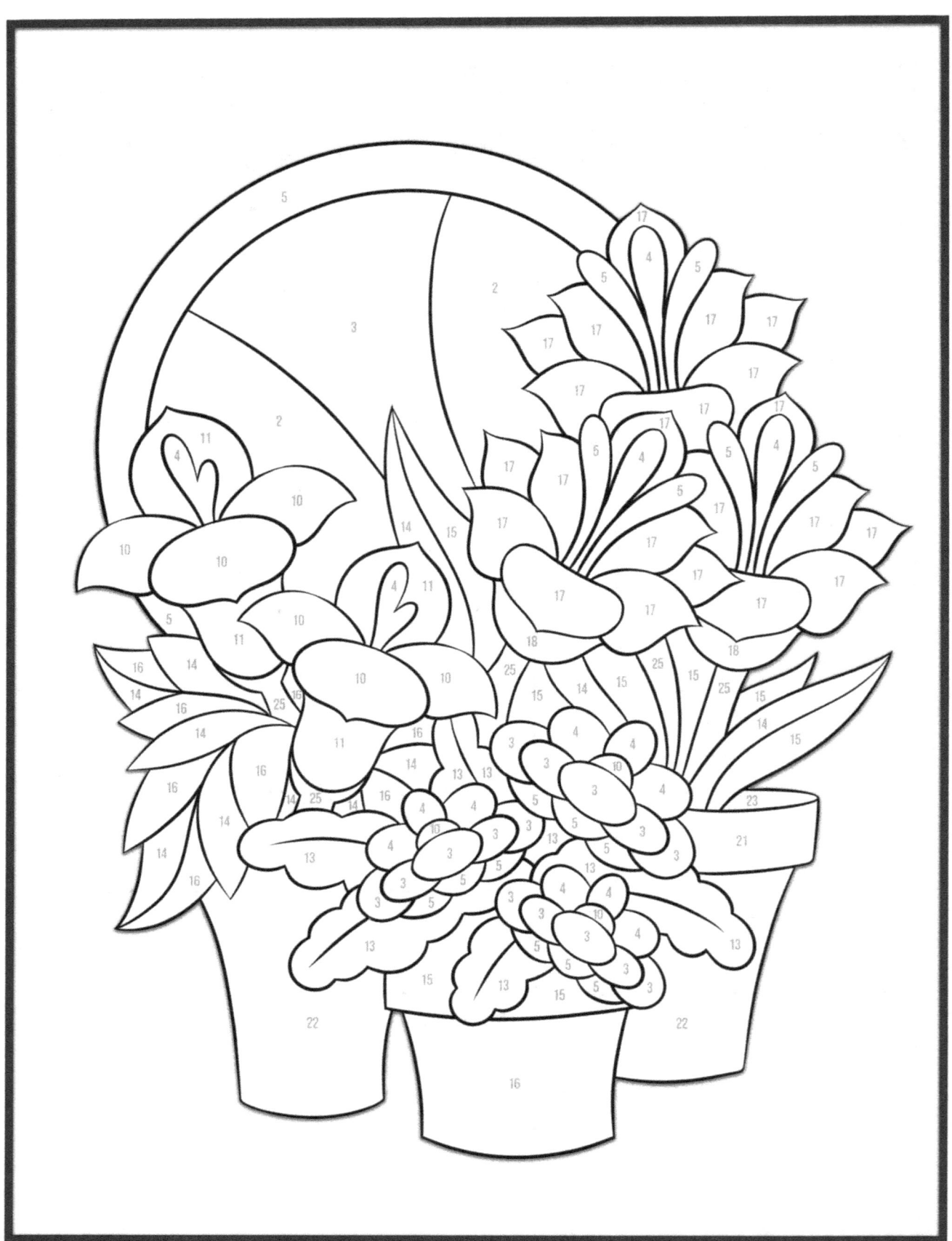

CUSTOM COLOR CHART

1. WHITE

2. LIGHT YELLOW

3. MEDIUM YELLOW

4. DARK YELLOW

5. YELLOW ORANGE

6. LIGHT ORANGE

7. MEDIUM ORANGE

8. DARK ORANGE

9. ORANGE RED

10. PINK

11. MEDIUM RED

12. DARK RED

13. LIGHT GREEN

14. MEDIUM GREEN

15. DARK GREEN

16. GREEN BLUE

17. LIGHT BLUE

18. MEDIUM BLUE

19. DARK BLUE

20. BLUE PURPLE

21. LIGHT PURPLE

22. MEDIUM PURPLE

23. DARK PURPLE

24. LIGHT BROWN

25. MEDIUM BROWN

26. DARK BROWN

27. LIGHT GRAY

28. MEDIUM GRAY

29. DARK GRAY

30. BLACK

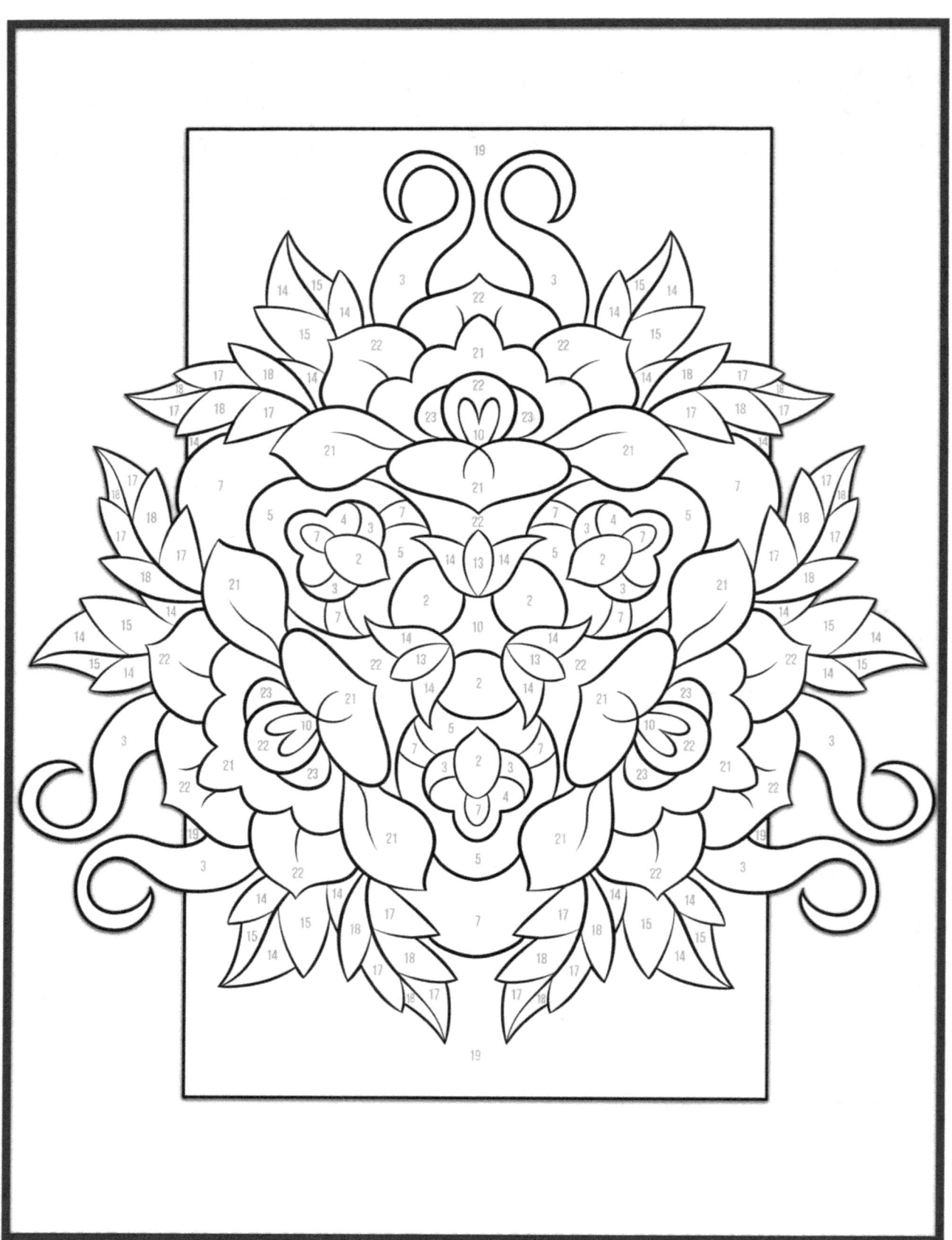

CUSTOM COLOR CHART

☐ 1. WHITE
_____

☐ 2. LIGHT YELLOW
_____

☐ 3. MEDIUM YELLOW
_____

☐ 4. DARK YELLOW
_____

☐ 5. YELLOW ORANGE
_____

☐ 6. LIGHT ORANGE
_____

☐ 7. MEDIUM ORANGE
_____

☐ 8. DARK ORANGE
_____

☐ 9. ORANGE RED
_____

☐ 10. PINK
_____

☐ 11. MEDIUM RED
_____

☐ 12. DARK RED
_____

☐ 13. LIGHT GREEN
_____

☐ 14. MEDIUM GREEN
_____

☐ 15. DARK GREEN
_____

☐ 16. GREEN BLUE
_____

☐ 17. LIGHT BLUE
_____

☐ 18. MEDIUM BLUE
_____

☐ 19. DARK BLUE
_____

☐ 20. BLUE PURPLE
_____

☐ 21. LIGHT PURPLE
_____

☐ 22. MEDIUM PURPLE
_____

☐ 23. DARK PURPLE
_____

☐ 24. LIGHT BROWN
_____

☐ 25. MEDIUM BROWN
_____

☐ 26. DARK BROWN
_____

☐ 27. LIGHT GRAY
_____

☐ 28. MEDIUM GRAY
_____

☐ 29. DARK GRAY
_____

☐ 30. BLACK
_____

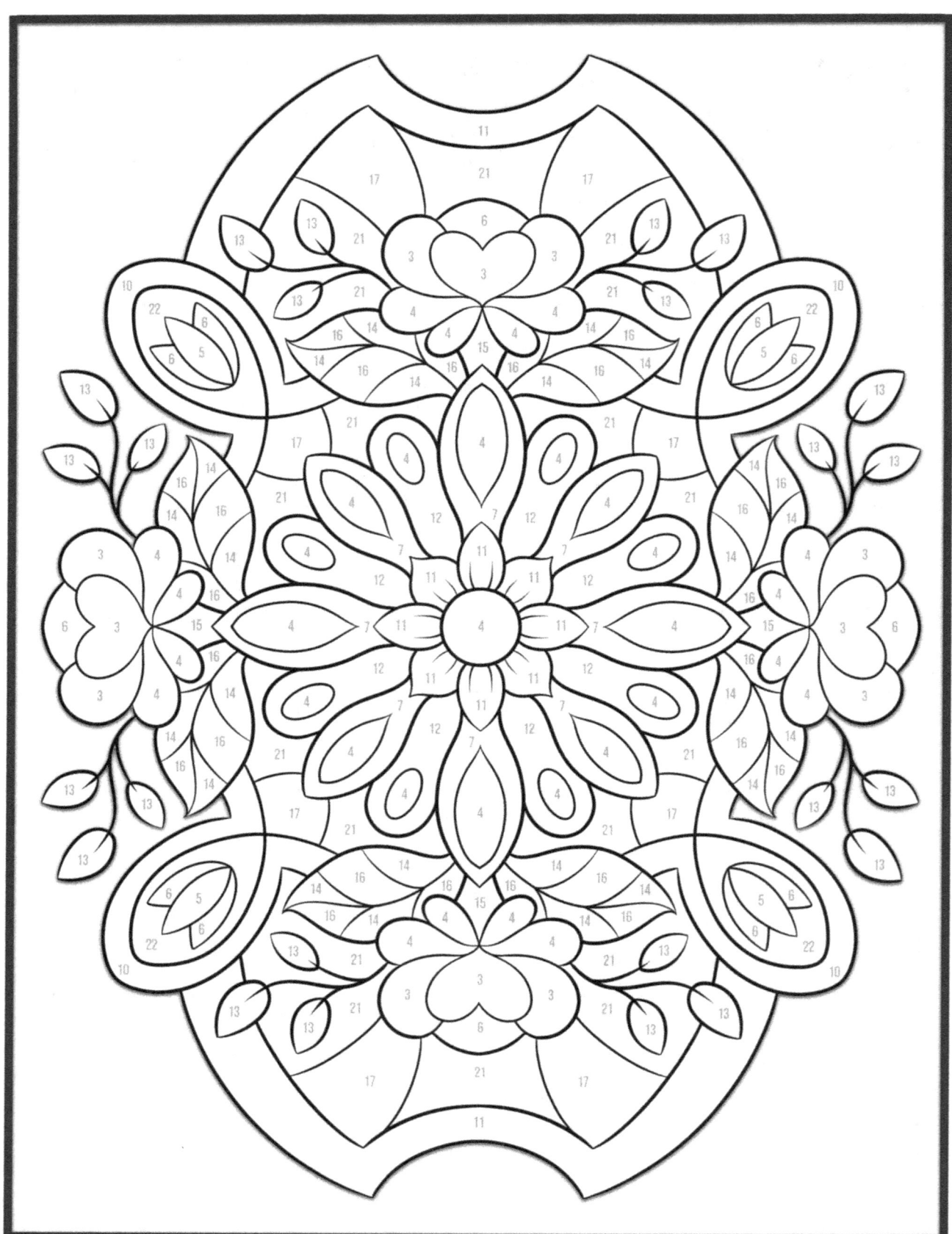

CUSTOM COLOR CHART

1. WHITE
_____

2. LIGHT YELLOW
_____

3. MEDIUM YELLOW
_____

4. DARK YELLOW
_____

5. YELLOW ORANGE
_____

6. LIGHT ORANGE
_____

7. MEDIUM ORANGE
_____

8. DARK ORANGE
_____

9. ORANGE RED
_____

10. PINK
_____

11. MEDIUM RED
_____

12. DARK RED
_____

13. LIGHT GREEN
_____

14. MEDIUM GREEN
_____

15. DARK GREEN
_____

16. GREEN BLUE
_____

17. LIGHT BLUE
_____

18. MEDIUM BLUE
_____

19. DARK BLUE
_____

20. BLUE PURPLE
_____

21. LIGHT PURPLE
_____

22. MEDIUM PURPLE
_____

23. DARK PURPLE
_____

24. LIGHT BROWN
_____

25. MEDIUM BROWN
_____

26. DARK BROWN
_____

27. LIGHT GRAY
_____

28. MEDIUM GRAY
_____

29. DARK GRAY
_____

30. BLACK
_____

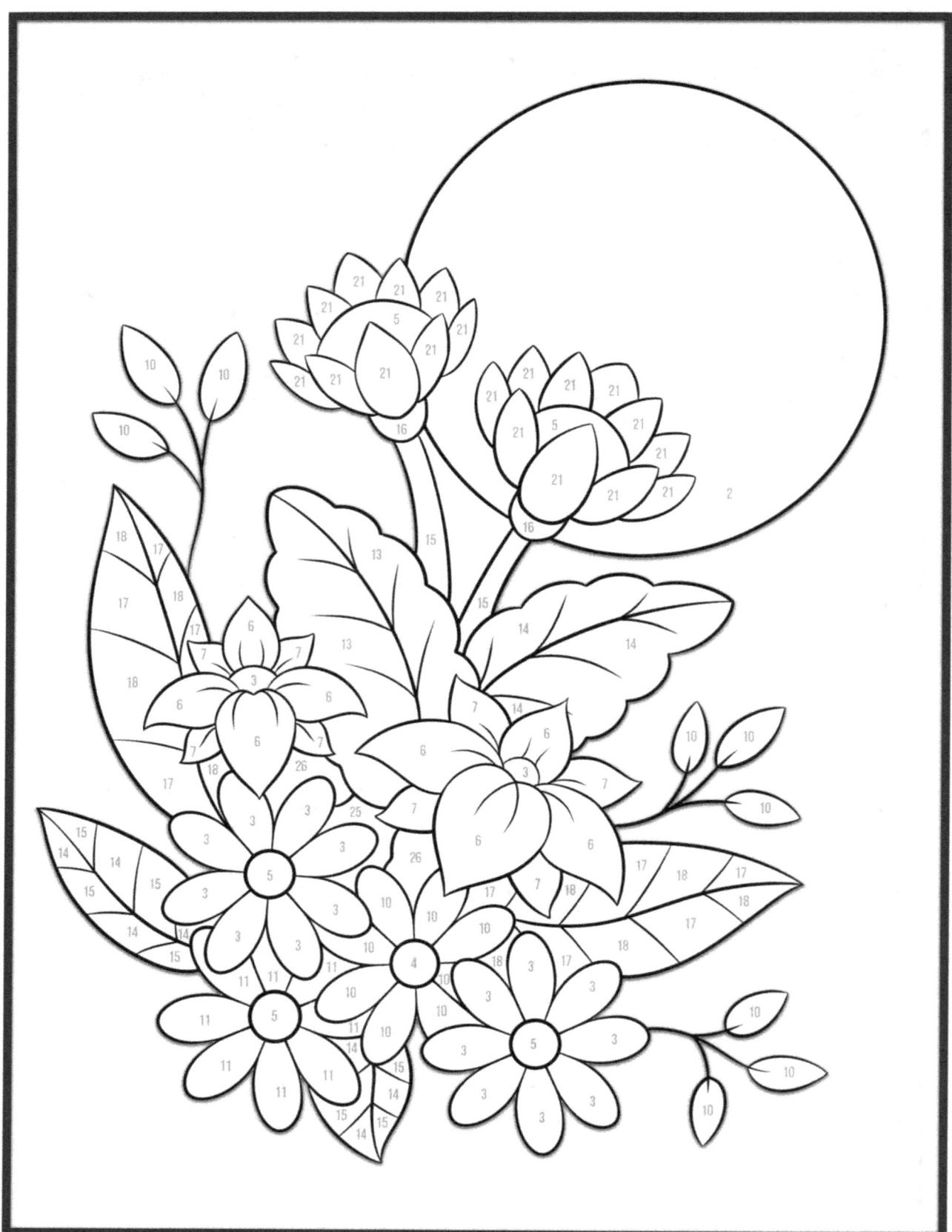

CUSTOM COLOR CHART

☐	1. WHITE	☐	2. LIGHT YELLOW	☐	3. MEDIUM YELLOW
☐	4. DARK YELLOW	☐	5. YELLOW ORANGE	☐	6. LIGHT ORANGE
☐	7. MEDIUM ORANGE	☐	8. DARK ORANGE	☐	9. ORANGE RED
☐	10. PINK	☐	11. MEDIUM RED	☐	12. DARK RED
☐	13. LIGHT GREEN	☐	14. MEDIUM GREEN	☐	15. DARK GREEN
☐	16. GREEN BLUE	☐	17. LIGHT BLUE	☐	18. MEDIUM BLUE
☐	19. DARK BLUE	☐	20. BLUE PURPLE	☐	21. LIGHT PURPLE
☐	22. MEDIUM PURPLE	☐	23. DARK PURPLE	☐	24. LIGHT BROWN
☐	25. MEDIUM BROWN	☐	26. DARK BROWN	☐	27. LIGHT GRAY
☐	28. MEDIUM GRAY	☐	29. DARK GRAY	☐	30. BLACK

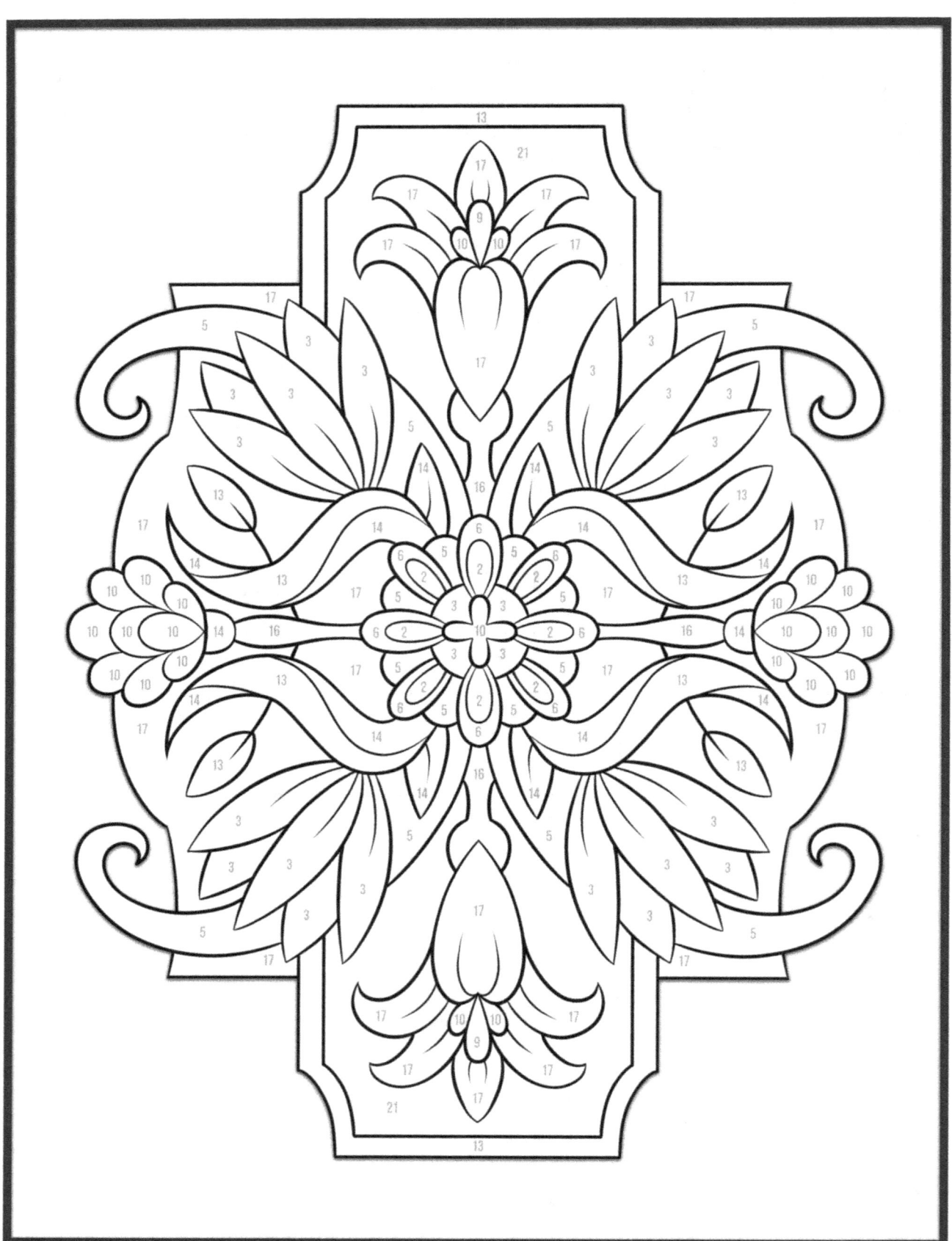

CUSTOM COLOR CHART

1. WHITE
_____

2. LIGHT YELLOW
_____

3. MEDIUM YELLOW
_____

4. DARK YELLOW
_____

5. YELLOW ORANGE
_____

6. LIGHT ORANGE
_____

7. MEDIUM ORANGE
_____

8. DARK ORANGE
_____

9. ORANGE RED
_____

10. PINK
_____

11. MEDIUM RED
_____

12. DARK RED
_____

13. LIGHT GREEN
_____

14. MEDIUM GREEN
_____

15. DARK GREEN
_____

16. GREEN BLUE
_____

17. LIGHT BLUE
_____

18. MEDIUM BLUE
_____

19. DARK BLUE
_____

20. BLUE PURPLE
_____

21. LIGHT PURPLE
_____

22. MEDIUM PURPLE
_____

23. DARK PURPLE
_____

24. LIGHT BROWN
_____

25. MEDIUM BROWN
_____

26. DARK BROWN
_____

27. LIGHT GRAY
_____

28. MEDIUM GRAY
_____

29. DARK GRAY
_____

30. BLACK
_____

CUSTOM COLOR CHART

1. WHITE
_____

2. LIGHT YELLOW
_____

3. MEDIUM YELLOW
_____

4. DARK YELLOW
_____

5. YELLOW ORANGE
_____

6. LIGHT ORANGE
_____

7. MEDIUM ORANGE
_____

8. DARK ORANGE
_____

9. ORANGE RED
_____

10. PINK
_____

11. MEDIUM RED
_____

12. DARK RED
_____

13. LIGHT GREEN
_____

14. MEDIUM GREEN
_____

15. DARK GREEN
_____

16. GREEN BLUE
_____

17. LIGHT BLUE
_____

18. MEDIUM BLUE
_____

19. DARK BLUE
_____

20. BLUE PURPLE
_____

21. LIGHT PURPLE
_____

22. MEDIUM PURPLE
_____

23. DARK PURPLE
_____

24. LIGHT BROWN
_____

25. MEDIUM BROWN
_____

26. DARK BROWN
_____

27. LIGHT GRAY
_____

28. MEDIUM GRAY
_____

29. DARK GRAY
_____

30. BLACK
_____

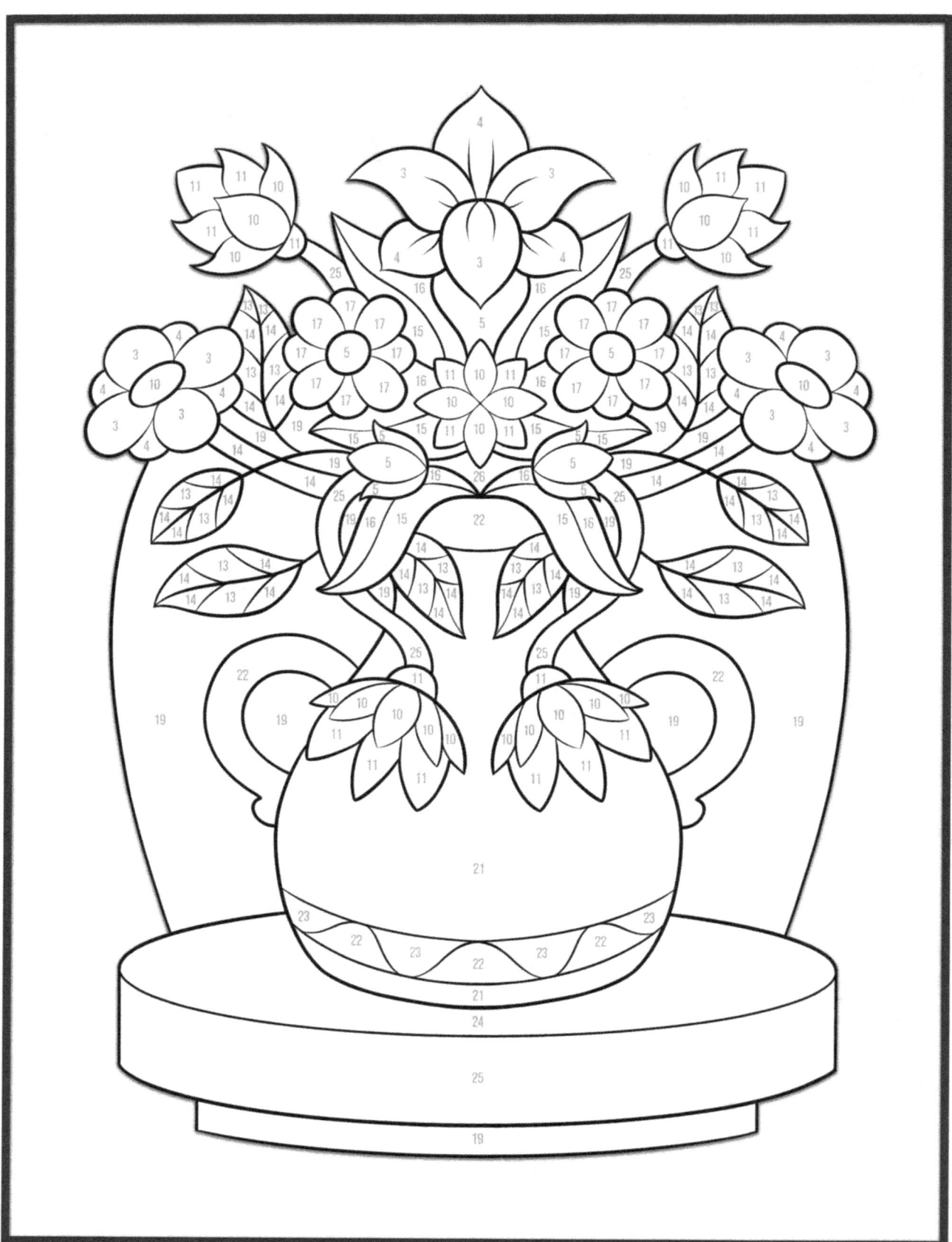

CUSTOM COLOR CHART

☐	1. WHITE	☐	2. LIGHT YELLOW	☐	3. MEDIUM YELLOW
☐	4. DARK YELLOW	☐	5. YELLOW ORANGE	☐	6. LIGHT ORANGE
☐	7. MEDIUM ORANGE	☐	8. DARK ORANGE	☐	9. ORANGE RED
☐	10. PINK	☐	11. MEDIUM RED	☐	12. DARK RED
☐	13. LIGHT GREEN	☐	14. MEDIUM GREEN	☐	15. DARK GREEN
☐	16. GREEN BLUE	☐	17. LIGHT BLUE	☐	18. MEDIUM BLUE
☐	19. DARK BLUE	☐	20. BLUE PURPLE	☐	21. LIGHT PURPLE
☐	22. MEDIUM PURPLE	☐	23. DARK PURPLE	☐	24. LIGHT BROWN
☐	25. MEDIUM BROWN	☐	26. DARK BROWN	☐	27. LIGHT GRAY
☐	28. MEDIUM GRAY	☐	29. DARK GRAY	☐	30. BLACK

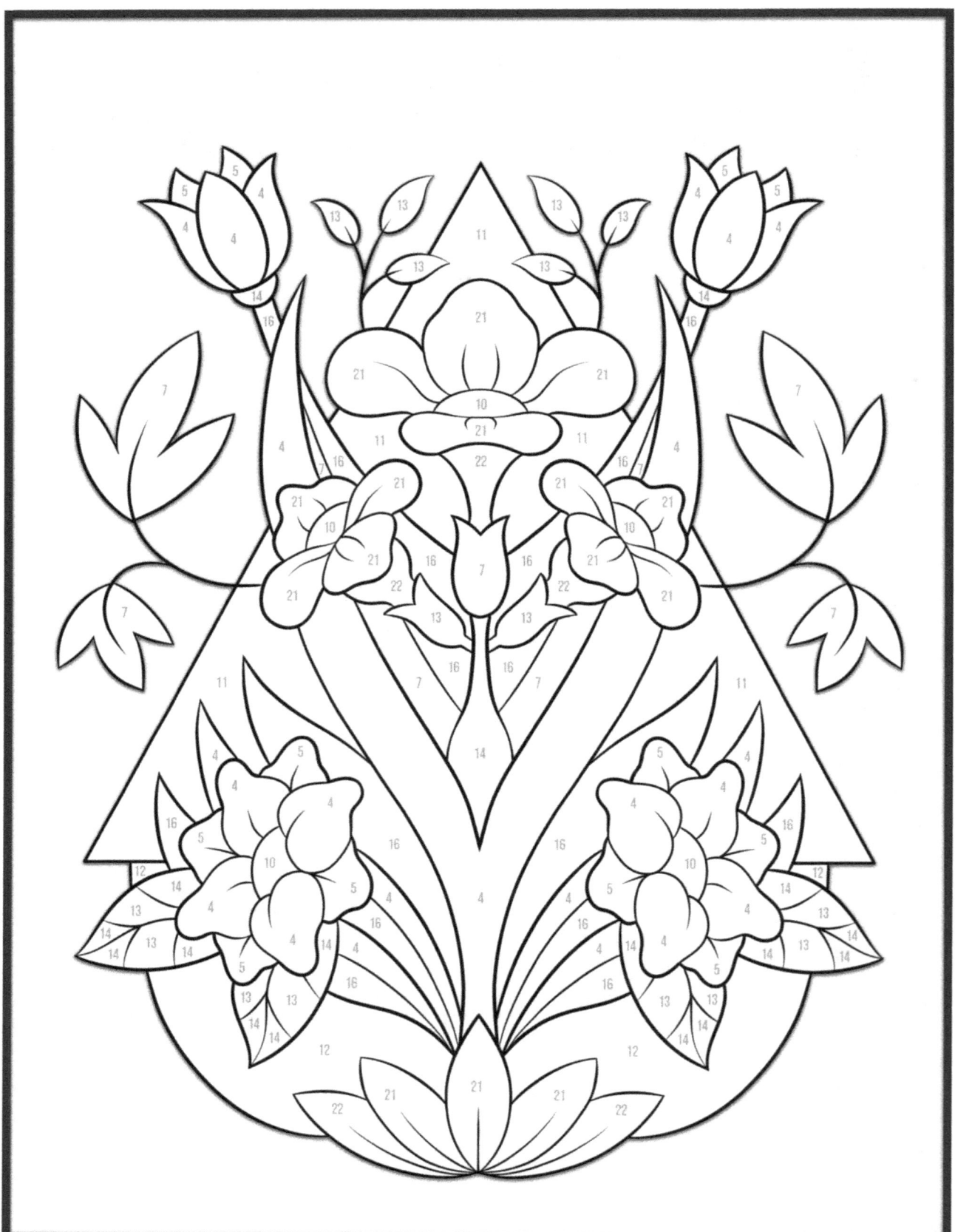

CUSTOM COLOR CHART

	1. WHITE		2. LIGHT YELLOW		3. MEDIUM YELLOW
	4. DARK YELLOW		5. YELLOW ORANGE		6. LIGHT ORANGE
	7. MEDIUM ORANGE		8. DARK ORANGE		9. ORANGE RED
	10. PINK		11. MEDIUM RED		12. DARK RED
	13. LIGHT GREEN		14. MEDIUM GREEN		15. DARK GREEN
	16. GREEN BLUE		17. LIGHT BLUE		18. MEDIUM BLUE
	19. DARK BLUE		20. BLUE PURPLE		21. LIGHT PURPLE
	22. MEDIUM PURPLE		23. DARK PURPLE		24. LIGHT BROWN
	25. MEDIUM BROWN		26. DARK BROWN		27. LIGHT GRAY
	28. MEDIUM GRAY		29. DARK GRAY		30. BLACK

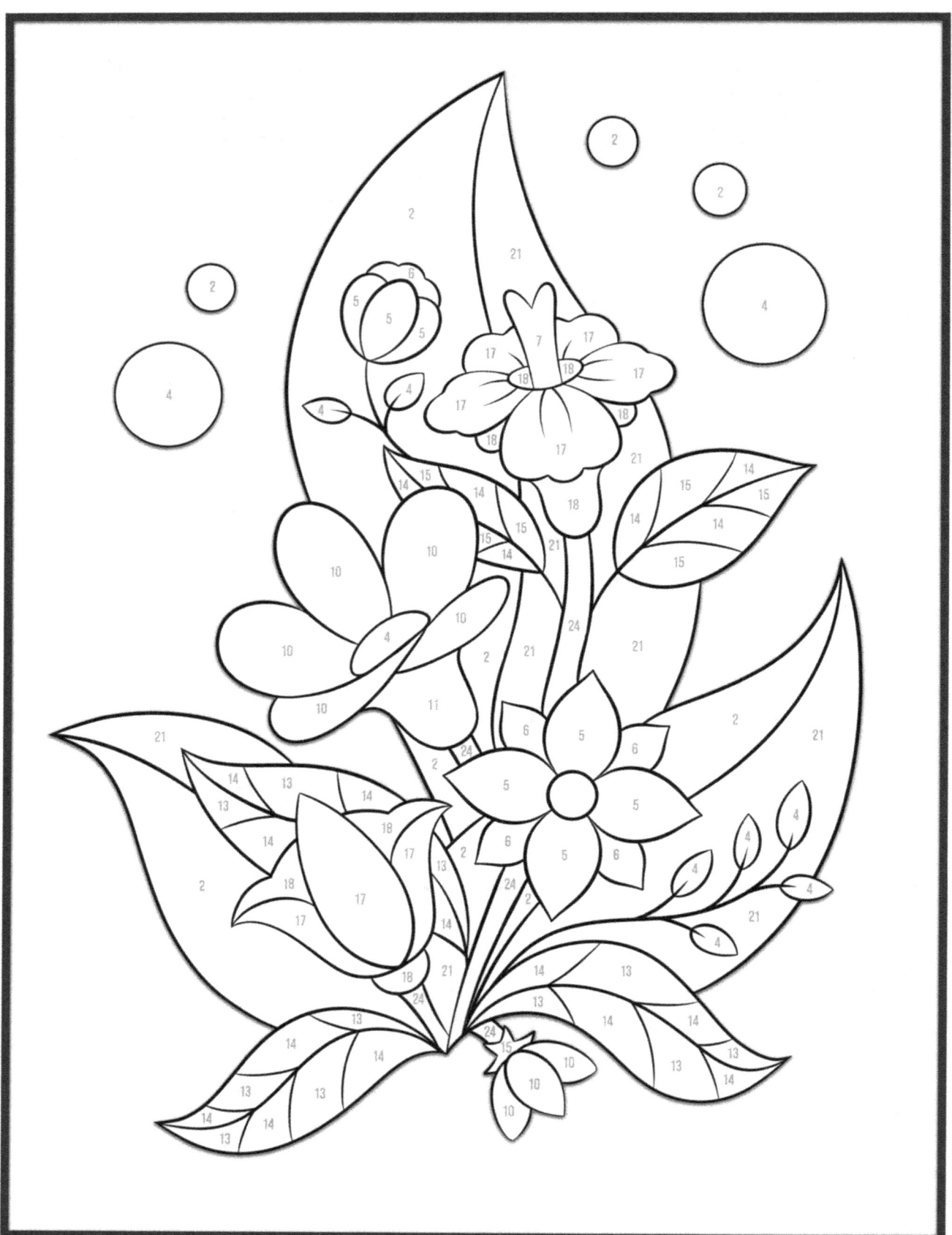

CUSTOM COLOR CHART

1. WHITE

2. LIGHT YELLOW

3. MEDIUM YELLOW

4. DARK YELLOW

5. YELLOW ORANGE

6. LIGHT ORANGE

7. MEDIUM ORANGE

8. DARK ORANGE

9. ORANGE RED

10. PINK

11. MEDIUM RED

12. DARK RED

13. LIGHT GREEN

14. MEDIUM GREEN

15. DARK GREEN

16. GREEN BLUE

17. LIGHT BLUE

18. MEDIUM BLUE

19. DARK BLUE

20. BLUE PURPLE

21. LIGHT PURPLE

22. MEDIUM PURPLE

23. DARK PURPLE

24. LIGHT BROWN

25. MEDIUM BROWN

26. DARK BROWN

27. LIGHT GRAY

28. MEDIUM GRAY

29. DARK GRAY

30. BLACK

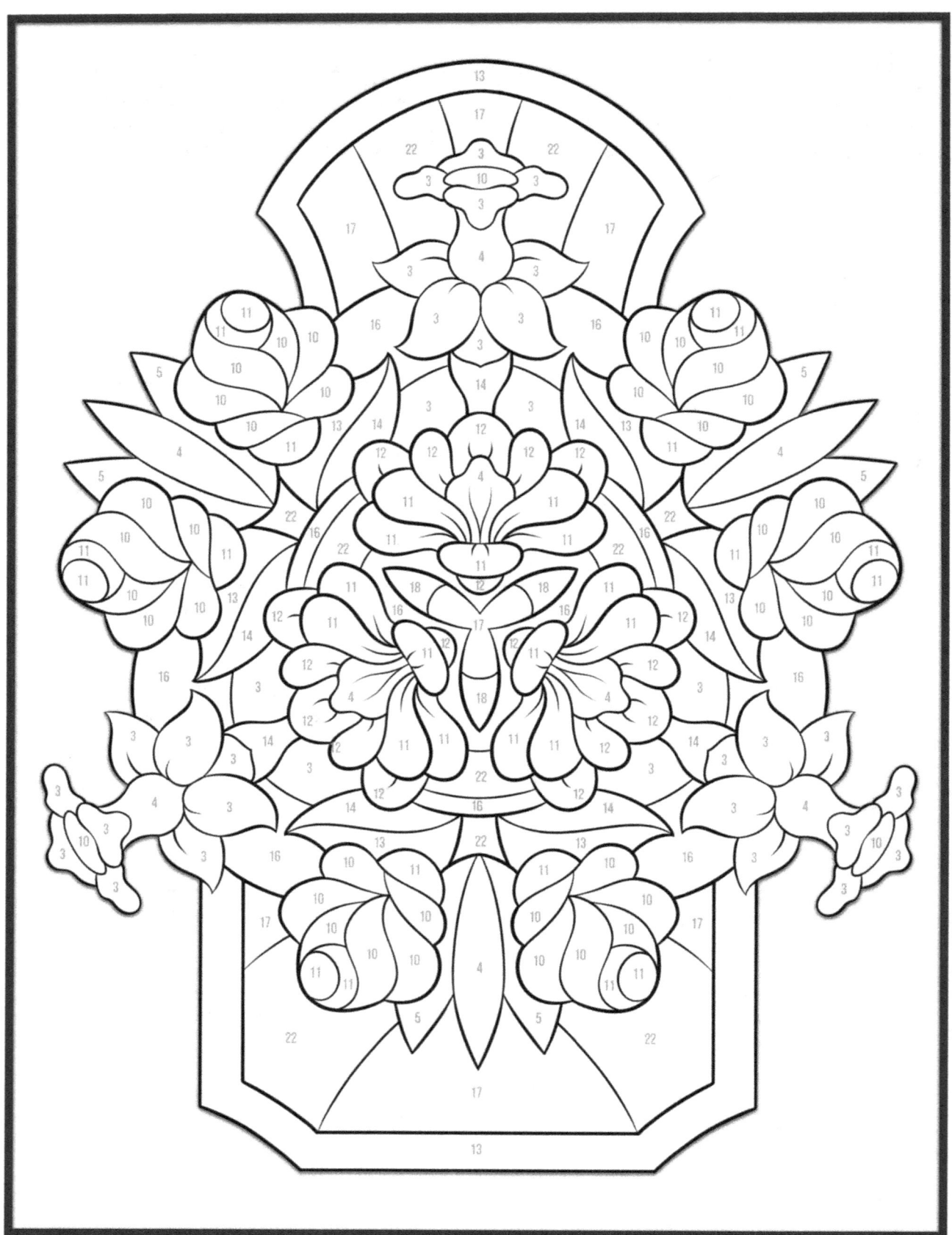

CUSTOM COLOR CHART

1. WHITE	2. LIGHT YELLOW	3. MEDIUM YELLOW
4. DARK YELLOW	5. YELLOW ORANGE	6. LIGHT ORANGE
7. MEDIUM ORANGE	8. DARK ORANGE	9. ORANGE RED
10. PINK	11. MEDIUM RED	12. DARK RED
13. LIGHT GREEN	14. MEDIUM GREEN	15. DARK GREEN
16. GREEN BLUE	17. LIGHT BLUE	18. MEDIUM BLUE
19. DARK BLUE	20. BLUE PURPLE	21. LIGHT PURPLE
22. MEDIUM PURPLE	23. DARK PURPLE	24. LIGHT BROWN
25. MEDIUM BROWN	26. DARK BROWN	27. LIGHT GRAY
28. MEDIUM GRAY	29. DARK GRAY	30. BLACK

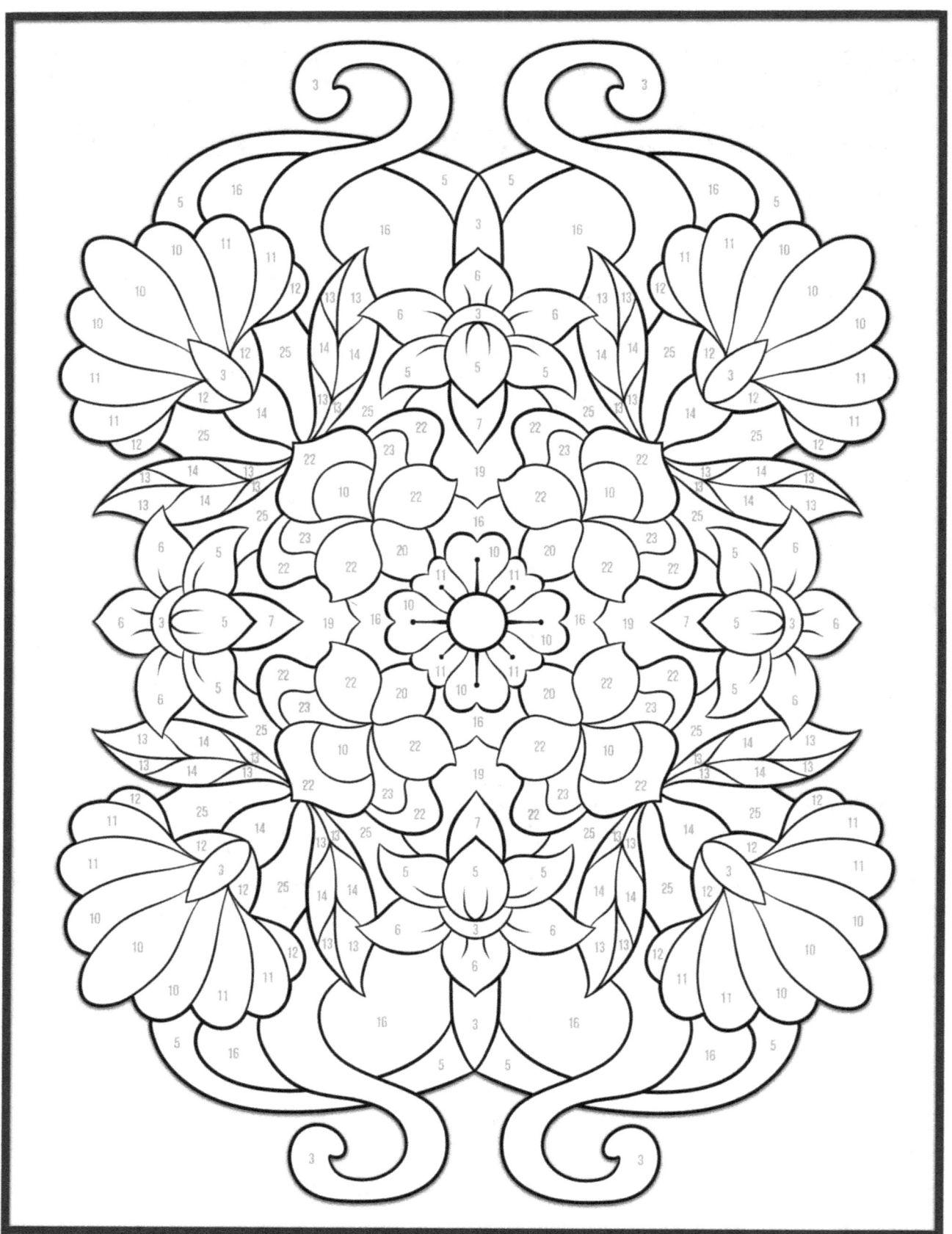

CUSTOM COLOR CHART

☐	1. WHITE	☐	2. LIGHT YELLOW	☐	3. MEDIUM YELLOW
☐	4. DARK YELLOW	☐	5. YELLOW ORANGE	☐	6. LIGHT ORANGE
☐	7. MEDIUM ORANGE	☐	8. DARK ORANGE	☐	9. ORANGE RED
☐	10. PINK	☐	11. MEDIUM RED	☐	12. DARK RED
☐	13. LIGHT GREEN	☐	14. MEDIUM GREEN	☐	15. DARK GREEN
☐	16. GREEN BLUE	☐	17. LIGHT BLUE	☐	18. MEDIUM BLUE
☐	19. DARK BLUE	☐	20. BLUE PURPLE	☐	21. LIGHT PURPLE
☐	22. MEDIUM PURPLE	☐	23. DARK PURPLE	☐	24. LIGHT BROWN
☐	25. MEDIUM BROWN	☐	26. DARK BROWN	☐	27. LIGHT GRAY
☐	28. MEDIUM GRAY	☐	29. DARK GRAY	☐	30. BLACK

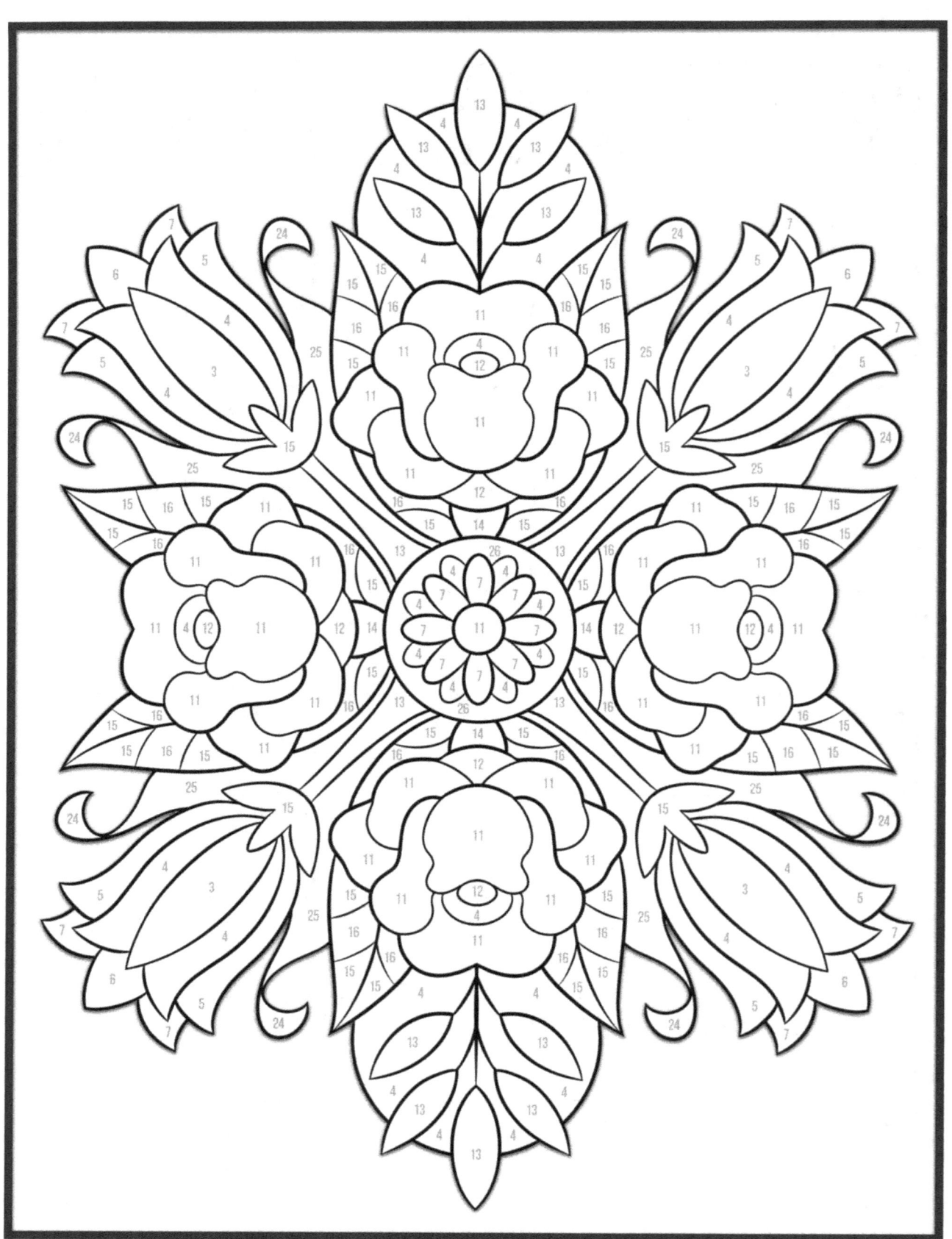

CUSTOM COLOR CHART

☐ 1. WHITE	☐ 2. LIGHT YELLOW	☐ 3. MEDIUM YELLOW
☐ 4. DARK YELLOW	☐ 5. YELLOW ORANGE	☐ 6. LIGHT ORANGE
☐ 7. MEDIUM ORANGE	☐ 8. DARK ORANGE	☐ 9. ORANGE RED
☐ 10. PINK	☐ 11. MEDIUM RED	☐ 12. DARK RED
☐ 13. LIGHT GREEN	☐ 14. MEDIUM GREEN	☐ 15. DARK GREEN
☐ 16. GREEN BLUE	☐ 17. LIGHT BLUE	☐ 18. MEDIUM BLUE
☐ 19. DARK BLUE	☐ 20. BLUE PURPLE	☐ 21. LIGHT PURPLE
☐ 22. MEDIUM PURPLE	☐ 23. DARK PURPLE	☐ 24. LIGHT BROWN
☐ 25. MEDIUM BROWN	☐ 26. DARK BROWN	☐ 27. LIGHT GRAY
☐ 28. MEDIUM GRAY	☐ 29. DARK GRAY	☐ 30. BLACK

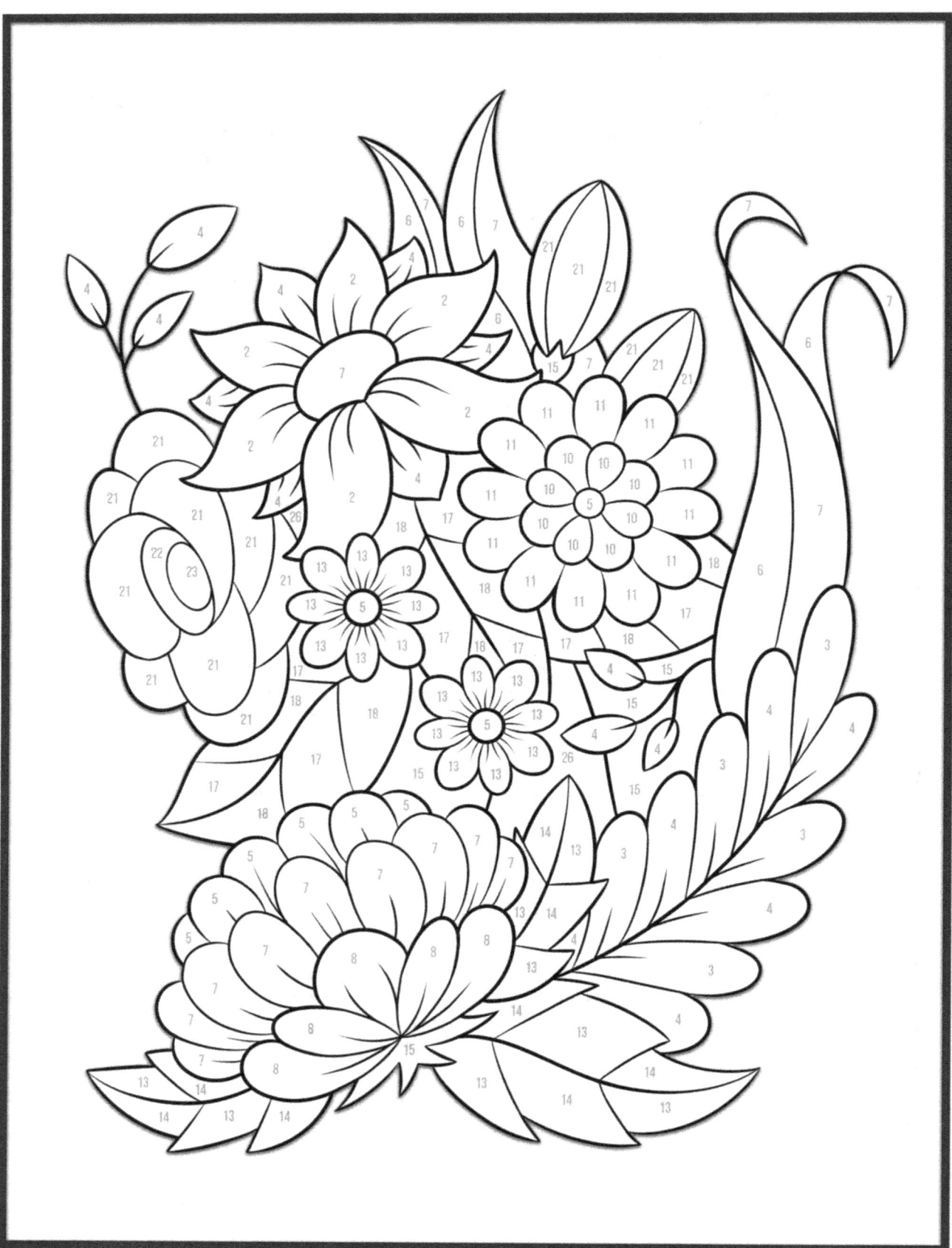

CUSTOM COLOR CHART

☐ 1. WHITE
_____

☐ 2. LIGHT YELLOW
_____

☐ 3. MEDIUM YELLOW
_____

☐ 4. DARK YELLOW
_____

☐ 5. YELLOW ORANGE
_____

☐ 6. LIGHT ORANGE
_____

☐ 7. MEDIUM ORANGE
_____

☐ 8. DARK ORANGE
_____

☐ 9. ORANGE RED
_____

☐ 10. PINK
_____

☐ 11. MEDIUM RED
_____

☐ 12. DARK RED
_____

☐ 13. LIGHT GREEN
_____

☐ 14. MEDIUM GREEN
_____

☐ 15. DARK GREEN
_____

☐ 16. GREEN BLUE
_____

☐ 17. LIGHT BLUE
_____

☐ 18. MEDIUM BLUE
_____

☐ 19. DARK BLUE
_____

☐ 20. BLUE PURPLE
_____

☐ 21. LIGHT PURPLE
_____

☐ 22. MEDIUM PURPLE
_____

☐ 23. DARK PURPLE
_____

☐ 24. LIGHT BROWN
_____

☐ 25. MEDIUM BROWN
_____

☐ 26. DARK BROWN
_____

☐ 27. LIGHT GRAY
_____

☐ 28. MEDIUM GRAY
_____

☐ 29. DARK GRAY
_____

☐ 30. BLACK
_____

www.ingramcontent.com/pod-product-compliance
Lightning Source LLC
Chambersburg PA
CBHW082139290526
45794CB00008B/3101